CHOICES BY T.B HUMAN™

CHOICES
BOOK 2.

by

T.B HUMAN

CHOICES BY T.B HUMAN™

CHOICES BY T.B HUMAN™

All rights reserved. No part of this publication may be reproduced, distributed, or transmitted in any form or by any means, including photocopying, recording, or other electronic or mechanical methods, without the prior written permission of the author, except in the case of brief quotations embodied in critical reviews and certain other noncommercial uses permitted by copyright law.
Printed in Australia and the United States of America

ISBN ISBN-13: 978-1-876776-07-7 (SC)
ISBN-10: 1876776072
ISBN **ISBN-13: 978-1-876776-08-4** (e)

Non-Fiction / Self-Help / Religion / Spirituality / New Age / Series

95,600 WORDS. approx

Published by TRUITY Australia
4 Crow's Ash Street Mount Cotton QLD Australia. 4165

CHOICES BY T.B HUMAN™

"It is impossible for a human being to stand in
the fire of passion
without being consumed by the flames."

– TRUITY

CHOICES BY T.B HUMAN™

CHAPTERS

Acknowledgements 8
From My Heart to Yours, With Love...........................8
Introduction 9
It all started at Number 62 13
Bitter Pill - an Email to a friend, 19th March 2003 ..16
PART 1 21
All Just a Game 22
Fast Forward...28
Thoughts of Reflection 32
Do You Know Where You're Going To?...................34
In the Beginning 44
First Light – New Life 48
The Search for It: Life on the Lonely Planet 54
Looking Back – The Intensity of It All......................62
Take a Pill and Hope It Will Go Away 65
The Way It Was 71
Is There More to Life? 77
On a Mission...80
Strength and Principles 82
The Quest for Meaning 84
Search for Truth 85
How Can I Get from Here to There?.......................88

The Need to Find Fulfillment 89
Everything Is Out of Season 93
Vision of the Future 100
What About Those Goals? 101
We All Came into Life to Heal Our Lives 110
Looking Back for the Last Time 114
The Aloneness 121
Turn It Around 123
The Search for Buried Treasure 124
Free at Last 126
It's All a Matter of Perception 127
Did It to Myself Again 130
Blocked or Not Blocked? 133
Fun and Games at Number 62 137
The Eternal Questions 143
Don't Pull the Wings off the Butterfly 145
Hang On; Help Is on Its Way 149
Going Electronic 152
Conflict of Interest 154
Home Again 157
One and One Make Three 180
Me, Myself and I 182
The Processing Obsession 188

Back Where We Started, But in Another World:
Caught in Groundhog Day 190
Walk a Mile in My Shoes 193
Another Clue 202
Start Spreading the News..209
The Lunar Eclipse 25th June 2002 211
All a Matter of Attitude 214
A Letter to a Friend, 7th March 2003 222
The Alien Connection 225
Somewhere Along the Path.....................................229
Karma, Karma, Who's Got the Karma?...................231
The Greatest Illusion of All 235
2003, a Year to Remember.......................................238
Predators on Mayfair: Monopoly Was Never Like This 240
Stark Naked as a Newborn Babe 244
Look Deep Inside 246
When Two Worlds Collide 248
Pitfalls on the Path 254
The Process 256
The Challenge of Faith...261
Endorsements 269

CHOICES BY T.B HUMAN™

Acknowledgements

From My Heart to Yours, With Love

My sister Marion, a huge heartfelt thank you!

My dearest friends, Lynne, Robert, Sally and Doug, Marilyn, Roslyn, Laurie and Mat, Gail and James, and Phillipa, have stood by me come what may.

Who can ask more of life than friends who love and listen even when they don't understand?

CHOICES BY T.B HUMAN™

Introduction

This manuscript is dedicated to all that have the courage to be honest and to have the faith and confidence to believe they can achieve what others believe and would tell them is impossible. I am not sure when I decided to begin this journey. It was probably the day I took my first breath as I was held in my mother's arms. I do know that life had to remind me that I had something specific to do in this life. However, I always seemed to be an oddity; I always believed that a person could do anything they set out to do. I just never realized how different my thinking was until I took up the challenge and set out to build an empire with nothing other than determination and courage.

I have always marched to the beat of a different drum, driven by a sense of spiritual insight which does not accept the limits others would have us believe are real. "Too far out there," many have said. I seem to challenge people just by breathing sometimes; I continually push the boundaries and defy the odds, keeping on where others have long ago given up. I have had to stand in the fire, never letting go of what I believe no matter what was thrown at me. I have faced the inner demons, the doubts and the fears, and the result is I have become all and more than I ever thought possible.

Many years ago, I was naive enough to think that if I were honest in every decision, if I had courage and learned the practical skills, them my life would become easier and people would respect me for whom and what I am. Since then I have discovered many things about life, not all to my liking, but one thing I have discovered as absolute truth is that our lives are simply the result of choices we have made.

Self-truth is something that we all know, and yet for the most part few have the confidence or diplomacy to embrace and follow it. Truth can, however, be identified. This happens when we read something and get that eerie feeling that we have read these words before. The experience is often accompanied by a spooky, uncanny sense of familiarity and *Deja vu*. Our truth is something we all have the ability to recognize. It is there in a sunset, in the words of a song, in the eyes of our beloved or in the silent reflection of the midnight hours when we lie awake alone in the darkness of the night. When it is absent, we feel the lack of it, as when someone is lying to us. Often, we know something is not right. We may not know what is exactly going on, but deep inside we know.

Truth brings with it a resonance that tells our nervous system that everything is all right. A lack of truth brings the jangling of a million cells to our attention, yelling at our inner knowing, "Listen to me. Something is wrong."

What has truth to do with choices? If we find the path to touch our inner truth, our choices are always appropriate and take us to our highest learning. I believe it is our innate nature for our essence to draw us towards our desires, to experience our potential and to live a life full of adventure, grace, and abundance. All we have been, all that we have the potential to be exists within our DNA. Our genetics hold the keys, deep within our subconscious memory and waiting to be rediscovered in this journey we call life.

Everywhere people are searching: searching for a sense of belonging. I call these people the "Wanabelong People." We all want the feeling of being at home and at peace in our own skins. People who are searching become involved in movements such as spirituality, New Age, religion, cults, metaphysics, and so on. Little do they realize the answer lies within. It's a matter of getting it right inside, as when truth resides without doubt, then things magically fall into place and we become our living potential.

I believe I have finally worked out why we experience what we do in our lives; I have found by experience that our healing comes not by chance but by choice. However, if you want to find out the secret I have learned you have to keep reading.

If you are on the path to your truth, you will probably find when you read this manuscript that it will seem so familiar to you. You will find that you already know the truth contained within these pages, and you may find

CHOICES BY T.B HUMAN™

yourself saying, "Yes, I know that." If that happens, then it is good, I have done my job. What I would love to hear you say at the end is, "It's all so simple. Why didn't I realize it before?" So many people today spend their lives searching for enlightenment, spending lots of money, trying new techniques and learning ways to control their nature, when in fact, it is the simple day-to-day interactions which hold the keys to experiencing all you could ever want. You see, the keys to a successful life are so simple most overlook them. This is the key point of my life, open and there for anyone to read.

My journey has bought me to my lives' work (yes, lives – many, many lives). My choices early in my life brought me to suffering, which gave me knowledge and experience which I then developed into my work, my career and my life. It is the empathy I bring to life which helps me help you. I do hope you enjoy BOOK 2 - *Choices*. Please read it with an open mind, and the next time you are faced with an awkward situation I trust you will realize that you, my friend, have a choice.
For those of you wondering, the word TRUITY means
TRUTH RESTORES, UNDERSTANDING, INCREASING, TRUST - YES.

CHOICES BY T.B HUMAN™

It all started at Number 62

Before I get too far into this story of the last few years, I would like to introduce you to a friend of mine, Lynne D., nicknamed "Secret Squirrel" or "Wallace." In the process of writing this story, some of my memories are being prompted by Lynne, my ever-loyal and longtime friend and personal assistant, as well as by the records of emails between me and David, my unlikely angel.

Why did we nickname Lynne "Secret Squirrel"? It started as a joke. Lynne has a talent for ferreting out information and finding ways of getting to people no matter who they are. Why the reference to Wallace? Well, if you ever sat and watched a story about Wallace Simpson and King Edward, you would surely see a striking resemblance between Lynne and Wallace, both in physical appearance and in their qualities as strong and elegant human beings. Lynne's naturally strong and eccentric personality reminds me of Wallace Simpson, as she even sounds like her. She has provided an enormous emotional support that has

CHOICES BY T.B HUMAN™

helped *TRUITY Choices*, and me, to stand the challenges of time.

Just the other day, I asked Lynne why she has stood by me through the tough times, thick and thin. Her answer was, "I would not be the person I am today, if I had not become involved with you and TRUITY. I cope with whatever life hands me now, and there is just so much I have gained, no matter how things turn out. It's that simple."

What else could I add to describe Lynne? Our Lynne, being a Gemini, has two sides, one of which, as I've mentioned a lot like Wallace Simpson and the other side a female version of Michael Crawford. I often think that if fate should bring the three of us together, we would get along famously. Lynne has a heart of gold; she is as stubborn as a mule and dedicated to truth, justice and righting the indifferences of the world. She is loyal beyond sanity and at times nutty as a fruitcake, with a wonderful sense of humor.

9th August 1998. I first met Lynne some years back while conducting a workshop in personal growth at my family's home in Annerley, Brisbane. At first meeting, Lynne was a shy, medium-frame, dark-haired woman in her late thirties, never married and with no children and yet with a passion and love for children that can only usually be found in someone who is a devoted mother of ten. Life had been giving her a bit of a tough time, and she had moved to Australia from New Zealand where she had lived for some years.

Lynne, like me, is English through and through. She told me a story once about how a pretentious psychic had told her that she had "ideas above her station" and should learn her place in life. Lynne, for all intents and purposes, could easily have stepped out of early nineteenth century gentry. It simply is her. She has an upper-class elegance internally at war with a clumsy prankster. She loves a glass of good red wine with, of all things, a cigar. Lynne simply appears to have brought with her into this life the energy of gentry. It is this sense of class which challenges many people and for some bizarre reason puts them off. To me this has always seemed quite odd really, but true.

CHOICES BY T.B HUMAN™

Bitter Pill - an Email to a friend, 19th March 2003

Robert, why is it that the world lives in such fear of stepping outside of the normal boundaries? Have you noticed how even everyday people have difficulty being honest and following through on commitments? I have been astounded at what I have experienced; it's a wonder that anyone achieves anything in this world the way it functions. On the business side of things, even though I have a financing contract for five million dollars, signed and assured in my hand, even my accountants will not help me through this difficult time. Is it because they can't really understand how I have achieved the outcome?

I have concluded that all the hard work and the years of persistence and effort mean nothing when it comes to people parting with their money. Not only that, but most people don't give a damn about helping the world lift its game and improve its ability to communicate; all they care about is the mighty dollar. Whatever happened to society?

CHOICES BY T.B HUMAN™

People look at me as though I am some sort of madwoman, just because I have lived my life with a passion to make this world a better place. And if one just happens to be outside the norm, they really view you with skepticism. You can almost see their thoughts of, "Where's the butterfly net?" I can only conclude that I have defied the laws of what others thought was possible and as a result I scare the hell out of most people with my commitment and persistence. They can't seem to handle that I am an ordinary person with an extraordinary commitment to do what I set out to do.

The accountants, on the other hand, appear to be so small-minded and so tiny in their vision that they even commented that because the investors are UK-based there was no way of knowing if they are for real. Can you believe that? Today, in this world of fast-track communication and global technology, many still try to function by old systems that just don't allow any space for the efforts and the abilities of the individual. It seems everyone wants a guarantee in life, but there are no guarantees, just as there is no such thing as security. All the money in the world, all the contracts and controls, can be blown away in a moment – bang – gone in a flash, yet people hang on to things and the illusion of security.

I don't know how anyone ever achieves anything, the way this world operates. I have always had the philosophy that if one door won't open then try another door; just keep on till you get it right.

Security can only come from our sense of inner confidence and trust. It's our ability to deal with whatever life hands us that guarantees success and fulfillment, and I don't think very many people realize that. It's strange that there is no measure to value people any more. Business has become dehumanized, and with that so many fantastic opportunities go begging. If I had the ability to change one thing it would be this element of business.

What a bizarre world it is. For the first time in my life I must hock my jewelry to pay for rent and food. Yet when next week comes and the money is in my company bank account, everyone will want to pat me on the back and say, "Well done! Weren't you lucky?"

CHOICES BY T.B HUMAN™

I bet the first thing they will ask is, "Now will you help me?"

Life sucks, mostly because of the lack of integrity, business etiquette and vision in the average businessperson. It would seem the world has it backwards, has lost its sense of humanity and fails to value the contribution of the person. Red tape and systems rule, and a person's effort and integrity count for nothing.

After all these years of defying the odds, I have come to that conclusion. I don't like the way people treat each other very much; there must be a better way. I think I will become a hermit and say, "Stuff the world." – At large. But I can't I just don't understand why it must be so hard! all my Love, Lesley

CHOICES BY T.B HUMAN™

PART 1

CHOICES BY T.B HUMAN™

All Just a Game

1993, Gold Coast Australia. The challenge was to create something that would use all my knowledge in a way that enabled people to be free and develop their own road maps to enlightenment. I kept having the words, "Personal development has to be more of a game," run through my mind.

People do tend to take life too seriously. After all, I had to be one of the most serious people I had ever met. For weeks I was oblivious to the fact that I had found the solution to this part of the puzzle. I felt as though I was suspended, hung in mid-air, just waiting for the insight to materialize. It's funny how sometimes we are so busy trying to find the answer to our problems that we just are not able to see things from another perspective.

A couple of weeks had gone by. One Sunday morning I was showing some of my latest drawings to a friend when he said, "Do you know what you've got there?"

CHOICES BY T.B HUMAN™

I looked at him blankly and said, "Not really. I know it's a drawing, and it symbolizes everything about what enlightenment is to me. But what do you mean?"

He was very excited and said, "You've got the key right there. Don't you see? It's a game. All you need to do now is to develop it." In an instant I was able to see the picture from another point of view. Instantly, what had been so elusive became apparent. My awareness changed in that moment, and goose bumps ran over me from head to foot. From that moment on, my excitement began to build, and enthusiasm immediately replaced the state of frustration in which I had been living. Enlightenment had arrived, and I was one step closer to being able to identify the process of it.

That is how the problem solving life game, called "TRUITY," was developed. From that point on, it was a matter of allowing the process of the idea to express itself through me, rather than my attempting to force its expression. In that moment, I began to become enlightened. By this I mean I started to understand where all the pieces of the puzzle would fit and finally started to understand *It*. Setting up the board for the game was easy. I had some insight into how the game would work, but I still wasn't sure how to get everyone to connect with whatever it was I seemed to do naturally. For days, once again, I wrote down all the insights and followed my gut feelings, not entirely sure what it was that I was creating.

I stretched my knowledge of brain function to the maximum. I found myself digging through boxes of notes I had made over the previous five years relating to physiology, stimulus and response, brain chemistry, attitudes, beliefs and personality traits. I scanned through my library of new-age books to see if there was another elusive ingredient which I could add to the puzzle. I understood I was creating a game which would teach people how to do what I had innately been able to do, but I was unaware of exactly what I was doing until I asked myself the right question. It had taken me all my life until that moment to learn the process hidden behind all human growth in consciousness. How could I find the question and then develop a process which would trigger its application for other people? My brain felt as though it would explode with the stretching and the mental gymnastics I felt I was undergoing. Mind map! I had to do a mind map that would help me discover what I knew that I didn't know I knew. And so off I went on another tangent of discovery.

Weeks later, the biggest mind maps you have ever seen was lying before me. The drawing was a masterpiece, a piece of art. But still the insight of how I was going to create the tool to help others grow and change eluded me. Insight came little by little over the next weeks, like little sparks of electricity accompanied by a feeling of "That's it," which would lead me on a journey of unbelievable growth and challenge. But for the present time there was still something that hadn't quite crystallized, something I was not seeing. There was one last piece of information still just out of reach. I kept thinking, "I know it is so obvious, but what is it I am trying to capture? What is it I am trying to identify so everyone else will benefit from it?"

What on earth is it? I paced the floor and meditated and paced the floor again. I used as much of my awareness and resources as could be mustered together and then I gave up. It was then that it all happened.

Yesterday, as I sat at my sister's computer, suddenly, the earth shifted. "Eureka!" I felt the rush of endorphins and the thrill that accompanies the explosion of understanding. However, this time even more than other times, I had an overwhelming sense of accomplishment and joy, all within the matter of a second. I got up and danced around the room saying, "Yes, yes, yes. I've got it." Something I had spent my whole life working towards was ultimately experienced alone. It was as though at that moment the culmination of all those years of work and study came to fruition, the key turned in the lock, and I once again did what I had done a million times before.

It was as if the nutty professor inside of me exploded in a starburst that lit up the universe for a moment. As all of this took place I realized and understood the process of how my brain can leap out of one perception into another. Once again, I had bridged the gap, and the unconscious became conscious. But more importantly, I realized how every person on earth has the ability to develop and achieve as much positive change and inner freedom in their lives as I have. The bewildering thing is that it is something we all already do; it's just that we don't know how to do it more often. For some people it happens on rare occasions, for others somewhat infrequently, for others frequently. The one common factor is that we all take it for granted. Finally, all the pieces fit together, all the study, all the insights, all the hours of contemplation. Finally, the hours in the labor room are over and the time of giving birth has arrived.

It was to be two long years before TRUITY was ready for distribution to the world market. Two years of incredible challenge, and once more against the odds, I have done what I set out to do. With no money, with no one to emotionally or financially support me, the universe challenged me to see whether I did believe in myself and my dream to the point where all doubt would disappear. Time and time again I was taken to the line with TRUITY. I would be at a deadline to pay my attorneys and not know where the money was coming from and the phone would ring, and there would be a gift or a loan of money to pay the costs. I stretched myself so far, out on a limb and succeeded simply because of my vision and love for humanity. The story of TRUITY is one for another book, another time, for to try to tell the whole story now would not do it justice. You will have to stay listening and watching for the next episode.

Fast Forward

From that day, on my life stopped, and TRUITY became my consuming vision. I had no idea how I would do it, but I knew I would. I had no idea what I had to do, but I knew I would find a way and my instincts would lead me. I just didn't know it would come with such a price. The price was to be my health, my relationships and my constant growth and self-exploration during the process. I would go to depths inside me beyond anything I knew existed; I was to feel such intense highs and depths of lows that I have no doubt if I weren't such a strong soul, I would not be here today.

While at that moment of realization I had approximately twenty dollars to my name, I would go on to raise the first one million dollars. I would learn about trademarks, patents, graphic design, writing, employing people, focus, emotional separation and more. My world was about to change, about to undergo a total cleansing of everything which was no longer appropriate. The end result would be that I would make space for my life to be renewed. I was about to become everything I always knew I could be, but it took thirteen years of weathering the storm to achieve that. People would walk away from me in droves, accusing me of being mad, altruistic, or incompetent; but those who stayed, my dear friends, saw my determination, my commitment, my belief in myself and what I had to offer. Many members of my family, many friends were lost to me along the way. My brothers, I have no doubt, thought I was mad, as I contravened the laws of the just-get-a-job world. I have no doubt they wanted me committed.

1998. The early morning sun flickers through the dark green leaves of the mango tree in the garden, as I sip my early morning cup of tea. It's as though my heart, my soul, my very essence is filled with a sense of harmony with life. For a moment, I close my eyes and turn my face to the sun, feeling the warmth, which fills my body with strength and life. Somewhere in the garden, hidden high in the branches, a tiny bird sings, each note carrying his joy to the world. A smile comes to my face as his joy of life fills every part of me. Not a day passes that I don't thank God for the peace which has now finally come to be in my life. For a moment in time I felt a small taste of sanity and peace that strengthened me for the further journey which lay ahead. I watch a butterfly as it delicately flits from one blossom to another, stopping to catch its breath, resting on the leaf of the tree, and I smile.

Off in the distance, I can see and hear the peak-hour traffic as all manner of people rush and bustle on their way to work. I wonder how many of them are happy with their lives. With a deep sigh, I acknowledge, despite it all, life does go on. If I gave you an orange, and you took one quarter from that orange, it would equal the portion of my experience I have written in this manuscript about my life. The events of my life have been so many, and the experiences so vast it is difficult to know what to include in this manuscript and what to leave out. If I wrote of all my experiences, no one would believe me, and sometimes I can hardly

CHOICES BY T.B HUMAN™

believe them myself. However, it is my understanding that we often spend far too much time focusing on the negatives of the past, when at any moment we can just let them go, and move on. To do this, however, we must let go not only of our physical clinging to the hurt and pain, but also of the beliefs and values which interfere with our perception of life. To be at peace and clear to make decisions, we must release not only the past but also our worry about the future from our minds, bodies and souls.

My life today is the result of all the hopes and dreams of my ancestors. Right now, I have the freedom to choose how I live and who I become. I have begun to understand what our journey into life is all about, and it is an experience I would not have missed for anything. The struggle and the pain have not been in vain, for they have given me the strength to reach out through time to understand how to live. In this moment, I represent the wisdom of all who have come before me and the dreams of those yet to come.

~~~

CHOICES BY T.B HUMAN™

Thoughts of Reflection

Today the world sits on the edge of war, the small-mindedness of man astounds me, as governments attempt to batter the opposition into submission. When will people realize that war is not a solution? When will human beings as a global family make a commitment to stop the violence? I must admit that when I look back at my timing for this whole project I am a little bewildered by the series of events, the coincidences, the timing – oh that word, timing.

I first noticed the coincidences when the Princess of Wales was killed in that tragic car crash in Paris, although I am sure they began long before that day. However, that was the day I had my stroke. I lay unconscious for 26 hours and no one noticed.

Since then it's been one bizarre coincidence after the other. For example, last year we put in motion a huge mailing to promote our company, and the day it was timed to arrive in the mail throughout Australia, terrorists bombed the twin towers. We have had numerous publicity events clash with world events, and mysteriously had mail disappear for nine months only to turn up after the event. Last week, for example, we were to prepare to sign financing contracts, and the United States went to war again, putting all our plans to move ahead on hold. One can only avoid becoming paranoid for so long then one must look at things and wonder what the hell is going on?

I once heard it said that each of us comes to our employment through our life experience, and I must say that for me this surely is the case. Thirty years ago, my life was one of total conflict. A war raged inside of me, one which tore apart my confidence, my life and my family, constantly erupting in violent outbursts as a result of the frustrations brought about by the lack of choices I perceived in my life. Thirty years ago, I made a choice to use my passion for life and the love I felt for my family to find away to stop the violence! This is my story, or part of it, for to write it all I would have to write a book so large that no one would believe the experiences it contained

CHOICES BY T.B HUMAN™

Do You Know Where You're Going To?

1994. The early morning light filters through the curtains and I toss and turn in my bed. It has been another sleepless night and my body screams with pain as I attempt to move my aching limbs to climb from the sweaty tangled sheets. Sometimes I wonder if the aches and pains which accompanied my recent illness will ever go away; there are times when it feels as though they are etched so deep into my bones that they are as ancient as time itself. Not to worry, being ill has certainly given me time to think about the past and prompted me to try to encapsulate all I have learned from my life experience this far.

With all my strength I struggle with the stiffness of my body as I lift my legs over the edge of the bed. God, I hate being ill! I find myself moaning out loud as put my feet tentatively on the carpeted floor as I make a grab for my dressing gown lying beside me on the chair in a crumpled heap. These days I feel as though my body is something foreign, not at all like I used to be, agile, fit and strong as any man. I struggle to take a few clumsy steps and catch myself feeling almost dismayed at how

CHOICES BY T.B HUMAN™

I must appear, 42 years old and walking like I am 90. Somehow the scene brings to mind how it would have been to have had my feet bound. Maybe I was a Chinese girl in another life. Who knows? I grumble out loud to myself, trying to block the pain from my mind as I waddle forward, forcing my legs and feet into motion.

Without being conscious of the fact, I begin singing the song which had been echoing round and round my head most of the last week, "Do you know where you're going to? Do you like the things that life is showing you? Where you are going to? Do you know?" It was as though I heard the words for the very first time. I stop in mid-stride, pushing my hair back from my face, almost frozen by the impact of the words hitting home within my consciousness as never before. I reach for the door archway and steady myself, my thoughts racing ahead of me. I once more begin moving towards the desk where my computer sits waiting, obeying the deep feeling inside of knowing it was time for another day's work to begin. I sit for a moment, seeing my reflection in the window glass as I search the early morning skies for inspiration and the strength to keep on.

My thoughts turned inward and before I knew it I was softly singing the words of the song, "Mahogany." As I sang I listened to the words, as if giving them permission to provoke thoughts about my life, and the ultimate question, did I know where I was going, and did I like what life was showing me? "Well I'm not sure; I think so," I half answered the puzzle of the words of the song.

I listened as my voice filled the silence of the room, as I gently sang over and over the words, "Do you know where you're going to? Do you like the things that life is showing you? Where are you going to? Do you know?"

The theme from the film *Mahogany* had been a constant companion of late, ever since I decided to take a chance and speak to someone about publishing this book. I had to admit I certainly didn't know where life was taking me; all I knew was there was no going back. I had finally shut the doors on parts of me which had been holding me back for a long, long time, or so I thought. My marriage of twenty-three years was over, my children grown, and for me, life was just beginning, so I thought. Even as I sat typing my thoughts, my life was being prepared, and I sensed the stage was being set for the grandest adventure of all.

Even during my illness, the preparation was almost complete, and the curtain was about to go up. Life was about to unfold anew. Wasn't this what I always wanted? I was single, free to do what I wanted when I wanted, with no one to answer to! For a moment I sat frozen in time pondering that very thought. Was this what I had always wanted? Hadn't I made my life exactly what I wanted it to be? Hadn't I always been driven to follow my path and compelled to search out the real reason why I was born? I never thought for one minute that my body would give in under the strain of the stress I was placing it under. Not for one minute did I ever think life would be like this!

I had searched for the answer for so long and I was so tired, tired of the searching, tired of the self doubt, tired of the loneliness and the feeling of not belonging anywhere. My thoughts spun swiftly, swimming and

CHOICES BY T.B HUMAN™

swirling through the memories which flooded into my mind. This world holds so much for us to experience. Why is it that some people appear to encounter one struggle after the other while others experience a blessed life? Why it is that some appear to be so ill prepared for the experience we call life?

Choices, it's all about choices, I began to mutter to myself. I never was one to be able to deny the truth of what I felt inside, I could not do one thing and think another; something within me demanded congruency, no matter what the cost. I appear to be born with such a strong conscience that often my bold stance has gotten me into all sorts of predicaments, just like now. A few years before I had become involved in what I loosely term spiritual practices. In other words, I began consciously developing my skills and abilities related to my intuition and psychic abilities. At the time I desperately wanted to find where I fitted in this world. I thought at the time that it was the way to find my place in it all.

Now in hindsight in the year 2003, I understand that every human being at some time in their life enters on the journey; we simply do it through different media. Some use education, some religion, some drugs, some music, and some spirituality. However, when you get to the bottom line, we are all looking for the same thing: a way to get life to work, and a way to live in peace and fulfillment.

Our life journey is simply our souls trying to fill our inner need to come to peace. Life is about the call to evolve, to develop our understanding and to understand our truth and that everything we experience is the result of the choices we make and the subtle subconscious needs and desires which influence our choices. If we are lucky, age brings us closer and closer to self honesty, and with the self honesty comes an unshakable trust in the truth of our intention and ourselves. In turn this leads us to live life in a much more peaceful manner. (If we are lucky!) It would seem, however, that there are some people who are not destined to become aware. There are others who seem to never ever wake to the other awareness; they just live a physical life.

CHOICES BY T.B HUMAN™

These people are not compelled by the same drive to become better tomorrow than they are today, and for the most part they believe they are alone and that when you die, you're dead, and it's that simple. And the irony of it all is that often a person who seeks self-awareness ends up married to someone who is not interested in anything to do with awareness.

Angels with lead boots on, souls who seek awareness but who bring earthly souls into their lives simply, so they don't fly off into the irrational unreality of a life like that of Alice in Wonderland. A small percentage of the population is compelled to ask "Why?" The whole journey of life for them is one self-development course after another. Every day is spent self-analyzing and searching the wisdom, which one day will help us become more and more aware of why life is like it is. People like me appear to be constantly challenged with the greatest obstacles, like being honest, having integrity, compassion, tolerance, and above all, faith and trust.

We believe there is some universal plan which binds us all together – every single person on earth – to some great plan of evolution. "Do you know where you're going to? Do you like the things that life is showing you?" I watch people around me astounded at the number who are just going through the motions of life, as though the destination is the important thing. But hang on. Isn't the journey the important part? Are you really living life or are you existing? Do you enjoy what you do every moment of the day, or do you keep wishing you were somewhere else with someone else? If you do struggle, what is it you're struggling with? Is it the search for love? Is it because you want more money, more power or more something than you have? Are you holding onto the pain of the past? Or in truth, are you engaged the eternal quest – the quest for freedom? Every thought you have creates your life, and ultimately your imprisonment or your freedom.

What is freedom? For me freedom is life! It's the ability to be oneself, the ability to stand in truth, the ability to love with respect and integrity, not only others but to love oneself. Humanity has searched throughout the ages, questing for enlightenment, using mystic rituals and chants attempting to control the elements of life, which create our existence. Yet it is said there is

CHOICES BY T.B HUMAN™

nothing more dangerous than a free man! Why? A person who is free cannot be imprisoned; their soul is untouchable, as they have found the essence of detached attachment.

My wise friend Arthur once said, "The greatest secret to life is to learn to live it – simply that. Enjoy every moment as if it's your last, spend time with people you love and show them you love them, walk in the sun and see the color of life which surrounds you. Live life, TRUITY; embrace all it has to offer in its banquet." Arthur taught me that when we live in truth we then live in freedom, and it's from this freedom that we build solid lives that lead others by example. Until we become aware we have a choice, many of our decisions in life are made for the wrong reasons. We make them to please others, or because we think it's what we must do. Often, we don't know we have a choice; we simply do the best we can with what we have. Then when we look honestly at our lives shock hits, and we realize we have not listened and honored the self, and as a result we often compromised our truth to have what we thought we wanted or feel safe or reach our goals.

CHOICES BY T.B HUMAN™

I had now reached the time of self-honesty; it had been brought on me through the circumstances of being ill. One thing for sure is that you take yourself with you no matter where you go in life, and sometime the universe must stop us in our tracks in order for us to reevaluate our lives. Only then do we make changes in our behavior and attitude. I had reached a point where I now had to face the realization that most of my life had been a lie. I had been in situations where I didn't want to be, but had stayed because I didn't think I had a choice. The result was that my body had become so stressed that my immune system had broken down, and I had contracted glandular fever and cat scratch fever, as well as something no one could identify. My life was falling apart around me; I could not go to work, I was alone, and fate was going to give me just enough time to reconsider my choices and to let go of whatever needed letting go of.

There were days when I often felt overwhelmed with sadness, and I knew a big part of my life was dying. I knew it was time for me to "wake up" and get on with whatever it was I had come into this world to do. I knew I could no longer ignore the calling. This awareness struck a resonance deep within me. I could no longer simply exist! Somehow, I had to take back my life, find my path, and above all, I had to become responsible and then from there to rebuild my life. Little did I realize that day just how far the journey was going to take me, or the enormity of the challenges I would endure. That Saturn energy in my birth chart, the teacher with the big stick, would accept nothing less than perfection from me in what was to come, and, my God, what a journey it turned out to be.

Ultimately, I was to learn that the price for freedom and peace is high. I had to be prepared to face the deepest darkest corners of my soul and stand in all honesty unafraid of the challenge in order to reach my destiny. The place of ultimate power lies within, and so the journey must begin.

In the Beginning

Little did I realize that in 1994, my journey was only just starting. I was naive enough to think that I had reached the destination, and that the worst was over. Finally, free of a bad marriage and answerable only to myself, I had to first learn to live life without a family to emotionally and physically support me. And then I had to work out how I would do what I wanted to do!

If I had only known what lay before me, would I have walked this path? I am not sure I would have had the courage; however, now that I am here, I wouldn't have missed it for anything. The person who struggled to the computer desk plagued with some unknown mystery illness was about to embark on the journey of a lifetime, or maybe ten lifetimes all rolled into one.

Life today in 2003 bears no resemblance to the life I led back in 1994. When I think about it, it's even further removed than I ever could have imagined from the day in the operating room in 1976 when my life force left me, and my world was rocked to the core when I stepped through the veil of life and death.

In that moment of death, my view of life in this world changed forever. With that experience, my views, thoughts, and understanding of spirituality and the evolution of consciousness completely altered. I begged not to be sent back to this world, but was told, "You know you have free will, but you must go back and finish what you went into life to do." What is fulfillment? I have come to the conclusion it is different things to different people, dependent upon what stage of evolution a person is embracing. Today I am a very different person from the person who began this journey. I finally have the courage and the knowing to be me, in every sense of the word, and life is just beginning.

I decided to rewrite my story, so the second edition of this story is very, very different from the first. For some strange reason many people have this inappropriate belief that when we become aware or enlightened then life will be simple, that nothing will touch us, and we manifest this surreal reality to live in. I want to tell you right now that this belief is complete hogwash. It doesn't matter how evolved we become; life still hands us the same challenges. Perhaps, in fact, it hands us more. The only thing that changes is how we deal with the challenges.

CHOICES BY T.B HUMAN™

I want to warn the enthusiastic beginner that the benefits which come from self-awareness and personal development are quite different from what people expect. If your life is not happy and fulfilling now, then be sure there are going to be a lot of changes before you find what you're looking for! Things must fall apart for them to be solidly rebuilt; it's like building a house. If you build on a poor foundation, then the house won't be solid, and it will eventually cost you dearly. The foundation I am speaking of here is the ultimate foundation for everything in our lives – and that foundation is truth. When you rebuild your life on truth, relationships improve, because you stop running all the old scripts. You enjoy each day as it comes and make every day something to remember, and the challenges which would have once sent you into a tailspin become mere irritation and inconvenience.

There is no easy fix in life. Becoming self-aware won't happen overnight but it will happen. Our lives are the direct result of how we think, how we process information, how we respond to circumstances and the choices we make. We can make informed choices, or we can simply run on autopilot and react to every little thing; it's up to us. I would like to think that my role in writing this manuscript is to help you be aware that you have choices, and to show you that there are other ways of looking at life experiences, and to reassure you we often only see a tiny part of the picture. For most of our lives, our actions are prompted by subconscious assumptions and presumptions, all of which are fed by our insecurities, fears, beliefs and values. From this cocktail of information, we unknowingly make the choices which determine how and when our lives will lead us.

The biggest problem we have as human beings is that we don't know what we don't know. We just do the best we can with what we have and blunder along, with all our past conflicts, confusions, and joys coloring our reality as we go.

First Light – New Life

1994. It's now the early hours of the morning, and with a cup of tea in hand and my trusty computer turned on, I settle back, preparing to write. My mind becomes a whirlwind of thoughts and ideas ready to pour into the computer. The next chapters of the manuscript are forming, taking shape in my mind and pushing to come forth on paper, the day's writing begins. For me to gain a different perspective on my words, I decide it would be a good idea to dictate my thoughts to audiotape as I write. When I listen to my words over and over it is easy to see subtle aspects that might require a little more explanation or an extra word here or there.

For just a moment my attention is taken away from the scattered pages of the manuscript, as the first brilliant rays of the sun's light burst forth in a cascade of golden beams of light over the horizon. I love to watch the sun rise over the sea; it's the most awesome sight – an inspiration of life renewing itself. I feel blessed with the gift of watching the majesty of the universe unfold for another day. The dining room where my computer sits overlooks the coastline of Queensland's Gold Coast. I sit in awe at the spectacular beauty; the dark sea is beginning to come to life, colors changing as the sun's reflection dances through the waves, merging with the flooding white froth, caressing the rock wall below my window. Off in the distance I can hear the drone of diesel engines, as the fishing trawlers move slowly up the Tweed River. The tide is just right for them to cross the bar, and I imagine the busy deckhands as they prepare for the day ahead. The hungry gulls squawk and screech, flying in circles as they follow the straggling team of tiny boats out to sea.

"All right, time to work," I mutter to myself, as once again the computer screen grabs my attention. For just a moment my body is filled with a feeling of, "Is this ever going to be finished?"

"Probably not," I mutter to myself. "A work in progress, yes, that's it. Life is a work in progress." I struggle with my old maroon dressing gown, arranging it comfortably to cover my naked legs, as the day's writing begins to flow from me, and I begin to read out loud the already completed pages of the manuscript.

As I begin to read the strangest thing begins to happen, from the moment my words begin to break the stillness of the morning air. It may sound quite strange to the reader, and it is my hope you will see the intended humor in the following. The professional guidance team told me that I am what is called a visual linguist. The universe gave me quite a challenge when I was born dyslexic. I began to develop my ability to express by painting and drawing. Words defied my ability to write them coherently, so I just drew pictures of everything I wanted to express. However, expressing with pictures was not enough for me, and from the painting came my desire and drive to find a way to communicate and create pictures with words. When you combine this with my passion to eliminate suffering in people's lives, (including my own) then there is one huge push to go against the odds and "find a way." We all have gifts, precious and rare. Writing and understanding people are mine; but just because I have developed these gifts, it doesn't mean it was easy. The challenge for me was to believe in myself, and just do it.

Life is often like a black comedy; my sense of humor, even in the most dreadful times, gives me the ability to laugh at myself and turn hardship into valuable insights. I use those insights to strengthen my resolve to achieve. I am, according to intelligence tests, a

CHOICES BY T.B HUMAN™

visual linguist – a word warrior, with a high level of creativity. I have a vivid imagination, and that imagination serves to bring me a balance between depth of insight and day-to-day reality. When I read a book, I see the story happening in my mind like a movie, in Cinema-Scope and Technicolor™. I have a sensory perceptual ability which is probably much greater than that of the average person, a "sensate," as the old terminology would call me. I feel and experience life so powerfully that often being in the company of some people is almost unbearable. Psychic and intuitive to the extreme, life has been a challenge, for knowing what you know and feeling the world so intensely takes a great strength and good firm hold on sanity.

This morning, however, as the words began to flow, somewhere off in the distance in the back of my mind I could hear the voice of John Clease, from *Faulty Towers*, reading my manuscript. It was as though I was listening to a radio station. "God, I'm really cracking up," I mumbled as a smile crossed my face. So, with great amusement, it was on that day I had the realization that life really is like an episode of *Faulty*

CHOICES BY T.B HUMAN™

Towers, and *It* never does turn out quite as you expect *It* to. Often when you look back, in hindsight all the drama and a great deal of the chaos was quite unnecessary and is all quite ridiculous. Yet I dared to question. "What is this mysterious ability we all must communicate with our higher soul, the ability to communicate upon multidimensional planes where time does not exist, and distance has no relevance to knowing what truth is?"

Most people would rather deny the presence of that ability for fear of being branded insane or even being other than normal, but we all have the same connections, some simply more developed than others. The sensory information is simply the mind finding ways to safely communicate information and translate that information from the unconscious to the conscious. The problems begin when people don't know how to understand what is happening or how to develop solid grounding in the midst of insight.

And so, with humorous thoughts in the back of my mind of life being like an episode of *Faulty Towers*, I began editing and retyping my manuscript, one more time. And once again the manuscript began to change, as I searched for words to describe the depth of my understanding of why we are here, and how to turn life into a wondrous adventure, filled with every possible experience, manifesting everything you could ever desire.

Back in 1994, my circumstances had given me a doorway of opportunity where I could do something different or I could sit and feel sorry for myself, so as usual I chose to make an opportunity out of a difficult time.

The Search for It*: Life on the Lonely Planet*

I have a sense that every soul that has ever been born or ever will be has something to contribute to the journey of this planet. I believe our journey is to experience life to the fullest, from every conceivable angle. What is the point of this experience we call life? Well, it is my belief that we come to learn the right use of will, and the right use of physical power, whether that is over another person or in reflection of our own experience. All the experience when put together creates a holograph of time and evolution like a giant multidimensional jigsaw puzzle. We are all a part of the one consciousness, with no division except those which our beliefs and egos create.

Every soul has come into life with an individual piece to add to life's giant jigsaw puzzle. Somewhere, somehow, in the midst of the experience we all call life, we all, sooner or later, discover that we all have something to contribute, that we to have a purpose and that purpose is unique to us alone. Each soul has been born with its own quest, the quest to understand, the quest to find solutions to the decline of our natural resources, the quest to make this world a better place, the quest to find inner peace and so on and so forth. Some may simply quest to find happiness or expression of their creativity. Or it could be the quest to solve the puzzle of that experience we call life?

However, from the very first moment we think to question, the moment we notice life is not how we imagined it should be, our journey has begun, and from that one moment of inner reflection, life will never be the same. That I guarantee.

CHOICES BY T.B HUMAN™

Now just because we have noticed something is not quite right doesn't mean finding the answer will be easy. On one hand, you have an aspect that yearns for answers. Yet on the other hand you have the *mañana* philosophy, or, "I will do that tomorrow; I am too busy today." It's quite a juggling act, and for even the most ardent seeker the challenge is to defy the odds and solve the mystery. As life demands, we stay totally absorbed in the confusion, emotions and beliefs that clutter our day-to-day lives. The worldly distractions, the passions, the needs and desires, as well families and mortgages and bills must still be dealt with.

These circumstances of our lives are all intricately intertwined with the clues to solving the puzzle of why we are not fulfilled and contented. However, our choices sometimes appear to be abandoning our families and heading off on some quest for the Holy Grail. Do we try to incorporate the changes in our daily lives and hope our partners will understand? Do we ignore the longing inside and simply do nothing? How do we juggle all the balls in the air without dropping any? How many choices do we have? What lead us to be here in the first place?

For some people the trigger which starts the search for self is prompted by the death of someone close; other times it may be that our own lives are threatened or shaken awake by some financial, physical or mental challenge.

A brush with death may trigger the sleeping human being to begin to awaken, but will it give the answers to why we are here and what it's all about easily? I very much doubt it. Maybe this world is only capable of being awakened by a natural disaster of enormous magnitude. Maybe there must be wars and catastrophes before people will stop and look at what is really important in their lives. Maybe when life is just coasting along we don't have enough pain to make us really pay attention, to make us want to change how we treat others and how we show our love to our family and friends. How much must happen before people take notice and decide to do something to help the consciousness of this planet lift and change?

CHOICES BY T.B HUMAN™

For the majority of the population, however, the strange sense of urgency increases only when the hand of fate touches our lives. Yet for everyone, deep within us all, the clock ticks away and the wrinkles and gray hair appear, and we watch as the calendar marks off the days and years of our passing lives. Days can never be relived, except in our memories. When we are young we tend to hide the urgency within us from ourselves by avoidance, compulsive behavior and generally too much of too much. We become workaholics, shop-a-holics or even alcoholics. But still within us all is an uneasy feeling and an unexplainable sense that we can't get "home" without finding or solving *It*.

And yet, what is *It*? Where is "home"? Why do I feel so unsettled and discontented? It's quite strange when you stop to think about it. If we are totally honest it's easy to acknowledge that for most of us, our lives consist of trying to control and arrange events to suit our vision of getting life to work. Some are lucky enough to naturally be able to go with the flow, and they have what would appear a blessed life; luck and circumstances smile on them, while others seem to struggle constantly. We all hope to finally unravel the clues and in doing so find a way to express our uniqueness and fill in the missing pieces, before we're too old to enjoy the benefits of the knowledge. It would be a shame to get to the end of our lives, and suddenly say, "I've got it; now I understand," just before you pop off.

Meanwhile, we go about our daily lives, the clock ticks and the hours pass us by, never to return. Somehow till now we have avoided facing the deepest questions, the needs, the passions unfulfilled. We hide these truths even from ourselves, denying their existence, like hiding a piece of a childhood puzzle from our brother or sister. Our destiny sits silently waiting, safely tucked away, just waiting for us to allow a flicker of introspection to spark its presence. One moment of self-reflection is all it takes; Pandora's Box is opened, and life will never be the same. Our personal development springs upon us with the fury of a hurricane. Just one second is all it takes to begin to stir the memory hidden deep within us. One second, that's all it takes for the journey to begin. Within us all lies a dormant distant memory of there being a better way to live.

CHOICES BY T.B HUMAN™

And with those memories comes the knowing that the potential of our soul to achieve is far greater than we ever could have imagined it to be. For me, my memory jolt came in the shape and form of a beaten-up magazine tossed in the corner of a doctor's waiting room. For you it could be hidden deep in the pile of things stuck away in the shed in the back yard. Or maybe it's buried deep among the stuff that grandma left you, piled on the shelf in the corner of the back porch. The memory could be stirred by the scent of a flower, the memory of a sunset or a child laughing. Anything can set your growth and development in motion at any time.

Of course, it's your choice, whether to listen to *It* or not. Daily we are bombarded by sensory information; the problem is that most people are not present to receive the information. They are busy in their imaginations and thoughts, and their thoughts are often lost in yesterday or exploring tomorrow. Little do they realize it is in this exact second, in this moment today that the answers are to be discovered.

CHOICES BY T.B HUMAN™

All too often our need for answers is triggered by painful experiences. The human psyche would rather erase or deny or avoid such memories, as the pain can sometimes be too much for one to endure. We are experts at carefully packing away things we don't know how or want to deal with, even though we know that one day we will eventually have to unpack them, face them and throw away what we don't need. The memories can be of unrequited love, or of loved ones who have passed away, sometimes tragically, or just too soon, or maybe during an argument that never should have happened.

The precious insights are held secret from our vision because the emotions and the pain are far too intense for us to be able to see past into understanding and wisdom. It is normal to feel overwhelmed by the enormity and complexity of life's hurdles. Trying to make sense of the confusion at the time something painful happens is often a fruitless task. We humans sometimes learn more when we look back than we do at the moment of confrontation. We have all heard it said that in hindsight everyone has 20/20 vision.

CHOICES BY T.B HUMAN™

Generally, most of us lack the skills necessary for questioning our perception of life's obstacles at the time of the challenge. We make excuses, in order to avoid having to acknowledge that we don't know how to deal with a problem. We say we haven't got time, so we don't have to stop and think and feel. We convince ourselves it is all right not to have time. Our priorities become unclear and we all but forget the importance of our loved ones in our lives. However, secretly we think, even if there were time, where would we start to fix things? The real problem often is that we don't know what choices we have. Our choices lie outside of our thinking patterns, so how do we find them? Books, training programs, religion, spirituality, education, and self-help groups, psychologist's r and counselors all present us with more choices. But wouldn't it be good if we could do all of that using our own knowledge? Wouldn't it be better if we could find a way to expand our choices, without having to pay lots of money or rely on other people? "There must be a way," I thought, and without knowing it, I had begun my journey. I had dared to question; I had dared to dream of a better way. Now what would be the challenges?

CHOICES BY T.B HUMAN™

Looking Back – The Intensity of It All

It was 1979 and the middle of a long cold winter's day. I was hurrying down a windy city street in Bathurst, when for a moment I was astounded at the sight of my own reflection in a shop window. I had been so deep in thought about the problems of my daily life that the sight of this gaunt, expressionless, lifeless face threw me completely. For just a moment I stopped in mid-stride as I caught a fleeting glimpse of someone I had not seen before, and I didn't like what I saw. For a fraction of a second the image changed, it was like looking through time. There was the beautiful happy face of a healthy young woman smiling back at me. In the blink of an eye she was gone again. I shook my head and found myself staring back at the thin, dark-haired woman. Who was the stranger with the gaunt face who had aged before her time? Who on earth was she? The deep shock of realization was almost too much, as I sensed I wasn't at all comfortable with what I saw reflected at me in the mirrored image.

Feelings stirred deep within my body so strongly, and the thought of dealing with them was far too much for me to bear. Maybe no one else would understand what it was that I felt, and maybe I didn't understand the presence of this feeling. This feeling of not being myself that accompanied me everywhere. Hurrying on, I pushed the thoughts back to the darkest deepest corners of my mind, mumbling to myself, "I haven't got time for that nonsense right now." My memories flashed back for a moment to my childhood and fleeting thoughts echoed with a memory. I remember that sense of her, I thought. Whatever happened to her? The girl who had such dreams and hopes? I never thought for one moment that life would turn out as it had for me. As a child, I spent many hours contemplating the universe. Even at the tender age of six I remember lying out on the grass at night staring up at the sky, wondering what was at the end of the stars. Confusion came when I thought, "But if there is an end there must be another beginning, and if...." It was just too vast to comprehend, and it still is.

The sense of something crept back upon me. It felt so strangely familiar; if only it could be explained or understood. The sense within my body was as though there was a deep memory, a knowing of something that was such a secret; I couldn't quite remember what it was I knew. I felt excited and scared all at the same time, but also bewildered. What utter nonsense, I thought, I'd better hurry home before the children get home from school or there will be hell to pay. That damn memory from childhood. What is it I am here to complete? What is *It*? When I tried to grasp a sense of *It* and my mind tried to recall the memories, it was like quicksilver, elusive. All that would happen is my body would fill to overflowing with a sense of excited frustration in response to the truth of that unknown elusive vision, a vision that would haunt me for many years. I had a vision, which I carried alone, and for me there was no one with whom to share my deepest thoughts. As time went by the unease within me grew each day. The restlessness and the longing to feel at home were calling me. The years just kept ticking by, and life went on.

Take a Pill and Hope It Will Go Away

1980's. I'll always remember that day of acceptance within me. It was no longer possible to avoid my feelings of confusion, of feeling like I was living someone else's life. The time had come to face it and embrace it. I had to find me and what I was born to do. Was it the tenth or twentieth visit to the doctor's? If my memory serves me correctly, I had been at the doctor's office at least once a week if not twice for the last few months. I felt utterly ridiculous, but my body felt so unwell and so tired, there had to be something wrong. It was the middle of the afternoon and I was feeling more than a little uneasy at facing the doctor once more. It was obvious the doctor would once again look at me blankly, and say, "I can't find anything wrong with you, Mrs. H, but take this medication to relax you, and see how you go. If this doesn't work, we will do some more tests. Make sure you come back to me next week."

I sat wondering why any of us are born at all. Is there any purpose to all the emotions and struggle we encounter? "What if the person I am is not the person I am supposed to be? Why do I feel so unwell all the time? Maybe if life had been different, I could be someone else. What if I am really someone else but I've never learned how to be that person? What if I

CHOICES BY T.B HUMAN™

have a purpose? What if I am not in the right place at the right time? What do I want to do with my life?"

How would I live if I could do anything? Who would I want to be? So many questions, and no answers.

At first, I rationalized if I could find *It*, then *It* would help me. Maybe it would help me to escape the worries and thoughts going around and round in my busy head. Maybe if I found *It*, then the confusion would disappear, all the problems of life would be easy to handle, and troubles would be far behind me. I didn't really know what I wanted to leave behind. Sometimes it was to escape the hurt and loneliness my husband stirred within me. Sometimes it was the boss or the mother-in- law; sometimes it was simply the injustice of it all, and the injustice that seemed to be surrounding my life. Yet at other times it was just the responsibility for others and the never-ending expectations and demands of being a mother and a wife Life was suffocating me. My life was wrapped with invisible strings that held me prisoner in an invisible jail. If only I could fly, far away from it all, and just live.

CHOICES BY T.B HUMAN™

But what was it that I longed to let go of? My thoughts raced. Life hadn't been going too well lately, but then I can't really remember when it had. There was never enough money to pay the bills, and buying a house while raising three children was totally impossible. Mack, my husband, was drinking more, spending more and worrying less. We had reached the point where our relationship was all a bit of a farce, really.

I tried too hard to be the perfect wife, hoping he would notice and want to spend time with me, to no avail. He seemed intent on avoiding me whenever he could; he didn't understand what was wrong. Mack's way of dealing with it was to withdraw and spend all the time he could away from the children and me. If my husband weren't at work then he would always find somewhere else to be, with his friends or off on his own. Life was so empty.

At that moment it seemed as though I worked to live, not lived to work, and every waking moment seemed to be a chore rather than a happy experience. My health was erratic to say the least. There was one mysterious complaint after the other, and secretly I was worrying myself to death. Maybe I really had some rare disease that the doctor kept overlooking. The strange thing was no matter how much I tried to escape my worries, my mind just wanted to keep on rehashing them, like a dog with a bone. It was so hard just to let go and be happy. My thoughts raced, and finding the solution to the puzzle seemed impossible. I searched my mind for a solution and in return I felt as though an avalanche of fears and doubts overwhelmed me. All the thinking, all the questioning, the entire struggle just seemed to be making things much worse.

During that afternoon in the waiting room I had the courage to take the first honest look at my life. All the confusion and outdated beliefs had to go. I had to find out how to be myself and let go of what society expected me to be. With this honesty came the extremely unnerving realization that I really didn't know very much about who I really was. The more I questioned, the more pressure and discomfort seemed to be building inside me. I was feeling like I was about to blow apart. It all just seemed so big, so overwhelming, I just didn't know where to start to fix things. I didn't know any other way to live except to

CHOICES BY T.B HUMAN™

take care of everyone else and that put my needs last on the list. Days were taken up with washing, ironing, cooking and cleaning, paying the bills, and so on. This wasn't how I thought life would be. It nagged at me so strongly it was like those blasted crossword puzzles, you know, when you're down to the last word and you know it but your mind just can't recall it, and you struggle, get frustrated and end up tossing the thing in the corner.

The bizarre thing was that in the midst of all of these thoughts I had wandered over to the magazine rack in the corner and picked up a rather tatty looking magazine. My eyes tried to focus, but my mind seemed to be intent on being elsewhere. The eternal question filled my mind: what am I searching for? What on earth is wrong with me? It wasn't comfortable being here. The doctor's office was filled with all manner of people, some old, some young, some spluttering and coughing and others looking just as miserable as I felt. After I picked up the magazine from the pile I quietly slipped back into my chair without really looking at anyone. I began to flick through the pages, and my eyes skimmed over the glossy pictures and the well-

CHOICES BY T.B HUMAN™

worn pages without really absorbing anything. I skipped a few pages, and just as I was about to throw the magazine onto the table, I noticed, of all things, a large scruffy crossword puzzle just a few pages from the back of the magazine.

There must have been at least a dozen different pens used to fill in these squares. Others before me had added their precious insights in an attempt to complete this particular puzzle. My eyes caught sight of one row of empty little white boxes on the page. There was just one line left to complete the challenge, but no one before me had managed to do it. I looked at the space number, and then back up to the reference questions for a clue to the missing word. Question 42: Use one word to describe the meaning and reason for your life. I searched my mind for the right word, but it eluded me. How peculiar. The question was exactly what I had been thinking about when I picked up the magazine.

The next moment a sharp voice broke my train of thought, calling, "Mrs. H, Doctor will see you now." I bolted from my seat like a startled cat and threw the magazine back onto the coffee table. A nervous smile flashed as I nodded towards the receptionist and headed through the doctor's open door. Instantaneously, I had been brought back to the reality of the moment, and my attention was once more consumed with just trying to cope.

The Way It Was

Looking back now, I recall that as a child growing up in the fifties and sixties, I was so incredibly painfully shy, so sensitive, and yet within me there was a strength and a questioning and, most of all, a deep sense of knowing. I wanted to create; I made puppets, and clay pots at the dam, went on adventures in the bush, sang constantly, and avoided people at all costs. I had no fear of the Queensland Bush and spent many hours wandering off climbing trees and having wonderful adventures. I didn't like people that much; they were nasty to each other, and I could never understand why they did that. My parents didn't treat each other like that, so why should other people? My parents, on the other hand, were so happy just with each other and us kids. They had all they needed right there, and until the day my father passed away, they still walked down the street holding hands. That is how I always thought life should be, safe and nurturing; I could never understand the way people were to each other. It always seemed so foreign to me.

There are so many funny stories about my childhood. My intuitive abilities were at that time unleashed, as I had not been challenged by the world about the reality of my experience. I had such a broad scope of experience to draw upon, and this supported and fostered a wild imagination. I would travel the universe and reach for the stars without ever leaving the safety of my deep kapok mattress. Looking back, I now realize that even at that early age my destiny was being set, creativity poured from every pore of my being. My adventure stories came to life in my paintings and drawings, and with words I wrote plays for my puppets, which I adored. I gave each puppet a name and personality, and I put on shows for the local kids. Poor Mum had to keep cleaning up my papier-mâché messes on the kitchen table, but she never complained. I saved my pennies to buy Plaster of Paris and paints, and whenever I could, more characters would appear in my wardrobe of self-made toys.

When I was about five years old, I went through a stage during which I was convinced I had been kidnapped and I had a twin sister who was blonde, and I told everyone I met that I had to find my sister. I did have a sister who died; however, she was two years older than I was, and she died at three months of age. I remember all I wanted was to go home to my real family. I have often experienced the overwhelming feeling of having been born into the wrong life and in the wrong circumstances. It's odd to feel as if you're out of place and in the wrong time. A part of my struggle has been to find a way to get back into that life and in doing so also find how to be myself within this life. The strange thing is that now I am blonde, and my eldest daughter is dark-haired, and much to her distress we are mirror images of each other. My early teenage years were plagued with insecurity. I always felt this was due to my family's move from England to Australia when I was three. My school years were overshadowed with our family's experiencing extreme poverty due to dad's having a bad accident. I also suffered with learning difficulties, as I had dyslexia and eyesight problems. I was happier with the animals in the bush and my pets than with other children and school. As I grew into a young woman, my lack of confidence compounded the deep loneliness I felt. We moved from the bush in my eleventh year to North Stradbroke Island, and my life changed, and there was nothing I could do about it. By my early teens I had already started to manifest physical illnesses because of not being able to communicate or escape my sense of not fitting in.

From the age of ten I always seemed to be sick with sore throats or kidney problems. No matter how I tried, I just felt I didn't quite fit in with other people. I couldn't understand why people treated each other the way they did! But how do you explain such feelings to those around you and not sound neurotic? I swam, I walked the beaches, I made a few friends and worked at the local cafe at night and on weekends, and I grew up way too fast.

My first encounter with violence came early in life. I was in high school, and in the evenings, I worked at the

CHOICES BY T.B HUMAN™

local cafe. One night while I was walking home from work I was attacked and raped. I hid what happened, not telling anyone, and just kept going as though nothing had occurred. The shame overwhelmed me, and I was convinced that no one would understand that what had happened was not my fault. I finally told my mother about the incident when she was eighty-two; she was astounded that I had kept such a terrible thing to myself all those years.

By the time of my sixteenth birthday, my natural talents for painting and art had begun to flourish. A tiny camera was already my constant companion, and artwork filled my room and visions of works to come filled my head. During most of my childhood money was scarce, and my family could not afford to send me to college, so I was encouraged to apply for a scholarship and to my surprise, I won. At the time my thoughts were filled with the dream of becoming a commercial artist, and for a precious moment life seemed to be offering me the golden hand of opportunity.

CHOICES BY T.B HUMAN™

However, fate had placed a different road ahead of me. During this time my romantic side was also flourishing at an incredible speed, and I had been dating a young man I had known for a couple of years. I was extremely naive in the ways of the world, and before I knew it, a new young life was beginning to blossom inside of me. My future was snatched out of my control as plans were made for me to be married a week after my sixteenth birthday. From that time on, it was as though my life took a turn in a direction over which I had no control. Life became a matter of existing; the battle was not just for myself, and it was now one of a mother and child's struggle to survive. The pain and confusion increased with every passing day. Sometimes being responsible and grown-up at sixteen was a little more than I could bear. By the time I was twenty-one, there were three wonderful children and a husband who spent most of his time either at work or with his mates. By the time I was twenty-six, I was suffering from ulcers, migraines, high blood pressure and cancer. When I was twenty-seven, I was confronted with the ultimate question of all, the choice between life or death.

CHOICES BY T.B HUMAN™

Is There More to Life?

I was only twenty-six when my cancer was diagnosed. A few short weeks later, with suitcase in hand, I entered a tiny hospital ward. Quite a safe operation, I was told, nothing to worry about. It was better to get it over with now than try to treat the problem with chemotherapy or radiation only to end up in the hospital again in five or six years. There would be no more children, which seemed more a relief than a problem. I could deal with that, I thought. As I was wheeled into the operating room, I felt an overwhelming terror. I was going to die; I knew it. Panic filled me as the anesthetic took hold and I knew it was too late, it was just too late. Who would take care of my children?

It was some hours later when, filled with panic, I struggled to awake from the anesthetic. Nurses surrounded my bed, and panic filled the room, my mind, my body, and my soul. The room swirled, and my thoughts raced fast. My head spun with a sense of floating backward and forward, in and out of reality. Panic filled my heart, and confusion erupted as my mind screamed with fear. What had happened? I was so confused. Every scrap of my body, mind, and soul was screaming, "No!" Where had I been? How could it be that I had been somewhere else? My mind struggled to understand what had just happened. My world; my reality had just been blown into a million pieces. Had that really happened?

How could a person feel such absolute love and why did he tell me I had to come back? If I tried to explain all this to the nurses I knew they would think I had gone nuts. I panicked inside and fought to try to contain my sense of chaos, no one could know what had happened. No one could know what I had just experienced.

My mind and heart were filled with the vision of a gentle man named Peter, with crystal blue eyes and hair like spun gold. His words like liquid honey echoed around and around in my head. "You know you have free will, but you must go back and finish what you have chosen to do." What did I have to do? What had just happened? The last thing I remember is panicking because I knew I was going to die, and who would take care of the children?

At the time my way of thinking didn't allow for life after death. I could only reason in my frightened mind, "If God spoke to me and sent me back, then I must have a lot of work to do, and a lot of debts to repay." I fought back the tears and pushed the confusion from my mind. There was no way I could escape the situation. Life had thrown me a curve ball, just when I thought I had it all under control. My reality had received the biggest wake-up call of all.

~~~

CHOICES BY T.B HUMAN™

On a Mission

That experience was to be the turning point in my life. I didn't actively begin to seek the answers; however, it was the point when my reality was shattered. It was from that moment that I understood I had a destiny; I also knew that what I had previously experienced as life was only a part of it all. How could I grasp the magnitude of *It*? The experience forced me to acknowledge that there was and is more to life. Questions began forming in the back of my mind, but I would push them aside. I felt as if I was exploding with confusion about what I had experienced. I had experienced it; it was just as real and just as valid as the chair I sat upon. Somehow, I had stepped through a door, a door to another valid reality, another world where more than anything the feeling – the memory – of love and of being "home" surrounded and filled every atom of my being. The experience was so powerful that to this day I can still feel and see it in my mind.

After my near-death experience, I felt even more alone in the physical world. I felt confused and afraid in a world where I did not belong, not knowing how to find the answers or understand "why me?" In those days, near-death experiences were not discussed as an everyday occurrence, and for me the choice was either to open myself up to psychiatric evaluation or just keep quiet about the whole thing and try to figure it out for myself. I chose the latter.

The result is that today I walk in two worlds. One is the everyday world, where it seems as if everyone is out to get everyone else, and very few see the truth of the love and unity of this experience we call life. The other is one of total knowing, without judgment and with acceptance of far more than I could ever put into words, a world where no one ever dies, where the souls of our ancestors are just as real and just as alive as if they never physically died at all. In those moments of my near-death, my belief with regard to "reality" changed forever. Without knowing how I came to the conclusion, I immediately understood that all of life continues to exist long after the body ceases to exist. There is no end to life, and the struggles we experience here on earth are but an experience we manifest in our journey to gain understanding of truth.

The challenges of everyday life are simply the way we learn to face our limitations and restrictive belief patterns. We come into the world with a limited perception; by the end of life we are supposed to have broadened that perception and gained understanding of the right use of will and how to live in harmony with those also sharing this reality. One can only stand in trust that one day we will all once again live in a world where hope and trust are for everyone to experience, everyday.

Strength and Principles

I was brought up in the Christian faith. I spent many hours wandering the Queensland bush, and found a sense of harmony there which has given me an understanding of the value of life and the nature of this planet. My mother always said God could hear you better outside in the paddocks, under the trees, and I believe she was right. It is man's need for power over others that has made a ritual of religion. Statues and idols are but a poor substitute for the reality I have come to know through my ability to be in tune with life.

The early years of my life enabled me to somehow learn a sense of intuitive depth that many people never understand. Being in the bush is at times a matter of survival by intuition; you just never know where that big black snake may be hiding. So, you learn to use your senses and listen to the nature of the earth. My family was comprised of my father, mother, sister and three brothers, all of whom are good, everyday people. We were taught to be honest, to have integrity, courage, and consideration, to be thoughtful and respectful and to honor those around us. My father and mother loved each other very much and were happily married for forty-five years. Their five surviving children are all very different from each other. Some have taken what life handed them and become a victim of it, sad, afraid and controlling. Others have just opted out. My older sister is somewhat like me, and I am the eternal optimist. All that life has handed me has served a purpose, and I have become strong and capable as a result, no victim here. As one friend said recently, "TRUITY, you are the eternal optimist, always in search of ways to create a better world."

The Quest for Meaning

After my near-death experience I was faced with a host of questions with no answers. Why was I born? Was there really life after death? How could I find out what I needed to do? Why was I more sensitive than the people who surrounded me? How could I turn my unfortunate life around, and how could I be healthy and happy?

Question after question flooded through my mind. I felt I was caught up in a hurricane of thoughts which followed me no matter how hard I tried to escape them. I still felt extremely restless and unhappy. I even felt almost tragic within myself. Countless hours were spent wondering what to do. I worked harder and harder, so I would not have to feel the pain and confusion or think about the experience. Then to add even more pain, my father died suddenly, and with his passing my already stressful life was thrown into absolute chaos. I felt as though my life was shattered into a thousand pieces. My best friend was gone, and for years to come the deep loss and unhappiness consumed me even more, and no matter what I did, or how hard I tried, life just didn't seem to work.

The more I tried, the more everyone expected; the more I gave of myself the more they wanted. I was losing all sense all sense of myself. I no longer had a life that was an expression of me; I lived for everyone else and tried to keep everyone else happy. Deep inside I just knew there had to be another way to live in the world; there had to be a way that people felt fulfilled and happy. Being the perfect mother and wife did not fill the hunger and the emptiness. Life just continued to be miserable.

Search for Truth

After that day in the doctor's office, life was never quite the same. Something in me had awakened. I could no longer deny the person who waited to grow and develop inside of me. I began by stealing only a

CHOICES BY T.B HUMAN™

few precious moments each day to ponder my situation and to tentatively explore the choices I had. My beliefs bound me within the experience and the frustrations of my world. It was an incredibly scary place to be, and there wasn't anyone to turn to for advice or to show me how to find what I searched for. I would wait until the house was quiet, the children at school, my husband at work. When I was sure I was alone I would settle down to write my thoughts or my dreams. I would hurriedly scribble notes into an old book, hoping first that no one would ever read them and second to find some clues as to what I could do to resolve this restlessness.

I always began by simply sitting quietly and closing my eyes and allowing whatever thoughts wanted to come into my mind, to just appear. Then I would begin to write. I didn't care whether it made sense or not; the important thing was I was beginning to express my deepest thoughts, and no one else had to ever know.

Sometimes there would be so many thoughts, they would all jumble together, and other times my body was so tired, sleep would fall upon me, and hours would slip away. It didn't seem to matter to me what happened, my intention was simply to be aware and watch my thoughts and see where they led me. It wasn't long before the first real clues began to emerge. For some curious reason my mind seemed intent on thinking of all sorts of crazy scenarios, most of which never actually happened. It wasn't long before I realized that I was at the mercy of an overactive mind. It was as though my thoughts ran me, rather than me being able to focus my thoughts. It was a bit like being in the middle of the city markets at eight o'clock on a Sunday morning, with everyone going in different directions all at once.

My thoughts were constantly about tomorrow or yesterday, and "what if" and "if only." It was quite crazy. Not only "What will people think?" but "How am I doing?" just kept crashing in. So, with my first realization in hand, I turned my mind to finding the next clue. At times I honestly began to wonder about my sanity. Did everyone think like this? If they did, no wonder the world is in such a mess. It was important for me to find a way to express all that I sensed inside. I knew I wanted my life to change. It was just too awful for it to stay the way it was. My determination pushed me on. The longing to be able to have the confidence to talk with people and to be happy was like a carrot in front of my nose all the way.

I still don't know how I had come to have such low self worth in the first place. Walking into a room with other people in it was just the most painful experience that I could imagine. Life was so lonely; the only company I had was my children and a good friend, Roslyn. I have no doubt that it was only the depth and the extent of the discomfort with my life that gave me the incentive to keep up my commitment to find a way to find *It*. The commitment was made, and somehow there would be time to spend a few minutes each afternoon just allowing myself to be focused upon myself without feeling guilty or afraid.

How Can I Get from Here to There?

There were many days when the whole thing just seemed too incomprehensible, too big, too hard, and my mind would end up screaming in frustration, "I give up. I'm not going to look any more. It's too hard. I quit." Within minutes, though, almost without any direct intention of my own, I would once again be thinking about what had just happened. I would find myself examining the last temper outburst and the irrational sense of hurt and rejection. Every aspect of my psyche would undergo a close examination in the coming years, and this was only the beginning. It was as though I was somehow on a train and there was no way of getting off until I arrived at the destination. It was like a magnet, which just kept on swinging back and forth until I faced whatever it was I needed to understand. *It* had to be a better life. Things had to be better than they were right here, right now. How naive I must have seemed during those days. Little did I know how painful, how hard, far and deep the search would take me.

The Need to Find Fulfillment

The restlessness and discontent seemed to grow within me with my every waking moment. However, the pressures of day-to-day life often prevented me from being able to place all my attention upon *It*. Life itself kept my feet firmly planted on the ground. Anger often flared, as family commitments stopped me from spending precious moments searching out my secret passion. My husband, by this time, was quite beside himself, and he spent more and more time at work or off with his mates.

There is no doubt in my mind Mack must have thought I was possessed by something, or lost the plot, when in fact I was merely engaged in a search for me. I often wonder what he thinks now when he sees the person I have become. Little did he know the bad-tempered, frustrated caterpillar was about to become a butterfly. All he knew was that he was losing the girl he had married; she was changing, and he was so frightened. His fears made him try harder to control me, and he was willing to do everything in his power to stop me. He didn't understand that the way to keep me was simply to love me. Instead, his mental cruelty and his need to control loomed larger than life, and our marriage slowly disintegrated simply from lack of nurturing.

CHOICES BY T.B HUMAN™

War was officially declared between us when I enrolled in a course to become a remedial massage therapist. He could not understand why there was a need to learn and become a little more independent. After all, isn't a woman's place in the home? All I wanted was for all our lives to be happier and to find a way to express myself. I honestly thought it would surely have to help. Surely, following my passion for learning would help me to find the missing pieces and to solve the puzzle. The study would challenge me, but it would also give me a sense of achievement and fulfillment, which my heart so longed to experience. The sad thing was there seemed to be no way to help him understand and give me support.

I kept a diary of my dreams and thoughts, writing every tiny insight down, no matter how bizarre it seemed at the time. The restlessness within me was like a cyclone brewing on the horizon, and as the storm intensified, the calling to find and fulfill my life's purpose became even stronger than my love for my children and my husband. Weeks and years had now passed since that day, and life was no better than it had been before. There would be brief moments when all seemed well, and then I would become bogged down and overwhelmed by one problem after another. My children were beginning to grow up and have their own issues to contend with; my husband would rather be with his mates at the pub or off fishing than be at home talking to me. Deep inside, I knew it didn't matter how hard I tried or how pretty I looked, nothing was getting any better. My sense of loss and confusion grew with each passing day, and the only thing that seemed make sense in this crazy life was my interest in spirituality and healing. The quest became my life, and it became the consuming fire, which gave me strength to carry on.

The stress and tension in my life was more than anyone could bear and sooner or later it was inevitable for me to find myself back in the doctor's waiting room. It was Monday morning and here I was again. I turned to the magazines on the table and I found myself faced once more with the same darn magazine. And still I found myself staring blankly at the empty spaces, wondering why no one else had been able to fill in that one word. I knew that I knew what it was, but the harder I tried, the more *It* slipped away from me. The doctor's visit went as usual. "Can't really find anything seriously wrong. Your blood pressure is a little high, and your glands are all enlarged. I'm sure it must be a virus, Mrs. H. Take this medication and if the symptoms persist, come back and see me and we will run some more tests."

The doctor smiled as he opened the door and ushered me out. There had been no enlightenment from the visit. I was still left to wonder why I kept getting sick, and why that stupid puzzle still hadn't been solved. What was the word to define the meaning of life? It was only years later in the midst of doing other things that, "Eureka," I got *It*. Somehow the elusive word to the puzzle flashed into my mind, and I hadn't even thought about it for ages. Just for a moment it was all so clear.

The realization happened with such speed, I could hardly catch it. I scratched my head and wondered why I couldn't see the simplicity of the answer before. For a fleeting precious moment, it all seemed so clear. Life was so simple, and then as quickly as the realization hit, it totally disappeared, and life went on.

CHOICES BY T.B HUMAN™

Everything Is Out of Season

By the time I reached middle age, I had already experienced many illnesses. Sometimes doctors put deadly labels on one ailment or another. I have a habit of looking at the core or essence of what we experience. For example, if you take the word "disease" and break it down, it is dis-ease, or a person not at ease with their life. Most of us experience some level of discomfort with how our lives manifest, but we feel helpless to change it. Obviously, I had a lot of dis-ease in the span of my life, and I was determined to change that. In the past I would have tried to force things to change. I used to monitor or pre-think the words and discussions over and over before I spoke them. I would only behave in ways which were deemed acceptable to others and show emotion only when it was appropriate.

I lost spontaneity and the ability to say, "I love you," to a friend. Such a spontaneous action was totally out of the question, as it might be something other than a genuine gesture of friendship. I made sure everything was in its place and there was a place for everything.

For some strange reason I used to think that if I could keep everything in its right order, then God willing, *It* or life would have to work. The harder I tried, the more energy and thought it took to keep it all in place, and the wearier I finally became. However, the need to find a way which does not take all this energy niggled at me until finally the quest or search for *It* once again became stronger and more determined than all obstacles. The need for inner fulfillment became the ultimate compelling drive within me, and that gave me the courage to move onwards no matter what the odds.

Many of my relationships broke under the tension, lovers became enemies and friends often become lovers. Finally, after our children had all left home, my husband left, too. For a while, my search turned outward. I tried to find satisfaction and fulfillment in the outside material world; I thought material satisfaction would ease the pain.

CHOICES BY T.B HUMAN™

Eventually, I had to face life on my own, and everything I believed had to go under the microscope. My life was not anyone else's fault; it was mine, and I had to find a way of being responsible and waking up to what I was doing which caused me the struggle and the pain. A lot of people only experience this sort of crisis in midlife.

However, such a crisis can happen at any age. For some, it's triggered early in life, maybe by the death of a friend or a life-threatening illness or a terrible childhood. For others it's triggered in their early thirties, when their working career is stable, and they have the usual mortgage and 2.3 children and two cars in the garage. Others find the empty nest triggers it, when the role they have been playing in life is over and their children now have lives of their own. Yet for others the penny drops just as they are about to get on the bus and leave this life. Things left unsaid, old anger and grudges are carried with them, life after life after life, until finally *It* is complete. Ultimately, we all see how those who have tested our patience so dramatically have loved us the most. We forgive them, and we finally learn to forgive ourselves for what we put ourselves through. Looking back on my journey, my perception has altered and expanded so many times I have lost count.

However, from this I have learned to be honest, especially in relation to my own motivation and expectations. Finally, and ultimately, I had to learn to take responsibility for the decisions and choices I made, all of which have led me to experience the pain of awakening and the challenge of learning new skills and the power of determination in holding my vision. The pain of the challenges was my greatest teacher, the unsung hero who volunteered to help me wake up and change and ultimately understand the whole grand illusion that we call life.

Once I thought there were lessons for us to learn in life; however, I no longer think that way. When I think in terms of lessons it creates a feeling of us all being beginners and inadequate in the grand plan of our evolution, and this belief creates a situation where we separate ourselves from the truth of life. Each of us has all the knowledge of all time. It's just that some of us have awakened or remembered more of our total consciousness than others.

The awakening will come to us all, sooner or later. It doesn't matter how it comes or upon which wind it is carried. It is as inevitable as death and taxes. We all, at some time, must contemplate the meaning of life. Hopefully, by the time we reach our deathbed we will have worked out what it was all about. If we are really lucky, we may finally understand *It* just before the conductor calls, "It's time to get on the bus. Next stop, the afterlife."

The enormity and complexity of the situations we all face in our daily lives can sometimes be so overwhelming it is natural to feel inadequate, but in truth we are fully capable of stretching the boundaries of our perception until the day emerges when we finally embrace freedom.

For each of us our life is the center of our universe. The word "universe" means "one song." So, in fact, we are the center of our one song. We will one day sing in harmony with all other living beings. When life is fine we don't bother to question or search; mediocre day-to-day existence has nothing within its structure to provoke change. Pain, especially the pain associated with love, is the greatest tool "God" or "Universal Consciousness" must get us to grow. I was once told there are three ways to enlightenment. The first is through suffering, and we all know that one well. The second is through acceptance; that is, when you just know there must be a reason for what is happening to you, but you just don't know what that reason is. The third way to enlightenment is through purpose. A soul with purpose is unstoppable.

Unfortunately, there aren't many of us who have such a strong sense of purpose that we will keep the dream alive no matter what happens. If you do dare to believe you have a purpose, the world would have you believe you are fooling yourself, and many will tell you, "It's just your ego." After all, if you have something important to do, maybe they should too, and often that is just too much for other people to accept. Most people are more comfortable going through life unnoticed. Their fear of responsibility is so great they avoid any opportunity to be different.

The majority of people never stop to think and really look deeply into the puzzle of life until they are shocked or grow into their own awakening. It's a sad truth that people often tend to wait until they are told they are going to die, before they begin to live. The thing that I find even stranger is often they don't realize that they have existed from day to day, instead of living. Each day is such a precious gift, so full of wondrous experiences to enjoy; life is for living, not existing.

Vision of the Future

I used to be able to imagine how my life would be in the future. Lately, the more I attempt to look into the future the less I can see of it, and yet the more I have a sense of where I am going.

In the beginning, I found feeling this way to be quite distressing. Everyone around me had goals and appeared to know what they wanted to be. There seemed to be a difference between the people around me and myself. I knew the type of person I wanted to become. They all seemed to focus on limiting goals. I just couldn't put my heart into the chase for material possessions. The things other people thought important and clung with a fear of losing, I couldn't have cared less about.

In my mind security would come from my ability to deal with anything life had to offer me, not how much money I had in the bank. By this time, I had everyone around me telling me to get my act together and accept my lot. People often said I expected too much from life. "Why don't you settle down, TRUITY, and don't rock the boat." All I could feel at the time was that life was just too hard. All I wanted was to be free. I wanted to have a happy, healthy life; I wanted to know how to get *It* to work, and I was willing to go through anything to get there. Whenever I compared myself to those around me I felt as though I was failing. I was just not like other people. It was inevitable for me to learn not to compare myself to anyone else, and that in itself was one of the biggest lessons of all.

What About Those Goals?

It was about one o'clock in the afternoon in the middle of the winter of 1984. I had been struggling with this thing about goals. I had been mentally tying myself up in knots and couldn't settle on any decision that felt right. My body was exhausted and miserable. It is easy to say that when something is your destiny, the internal natural force will keep steering you to take that direction. It is impossible to miss what is destined to be your destiny; however, it is so hard to hang on to at times.

We all seem to have the ability, once in a while, to tune in to an internal compass. However, whether we listen to it or not is entirely our choice. When we are in tune with the clarity and knowing, things just fall into place. I knew all this, but it was still so hard just to allow things to come to me, and for the universe to show me what to do next. I had no doubt in my mind that somehow, I was facing south when I should have been facing north. Every so often a little bit of magic would take place, and in the flash of an eye I would begin to be able to think about a situation from an entirely different perspective.

One afternoon I was lying on the bed, feeling like a failure once more, judging myself too harshly, when I found myself thinking about what would happen if I died tomorrow. Who would really care? How would anyone even know I had been alive? I had a husband who loved me in his own strange way; I had three children who would miss me, but so what?

It was one of the most profound moments of my life. I had a vision in my mind's eye of my funeral, and there were only a handful of people there. That vision created a feeling of extreme sadness, and along with it an incredible sense of knowing that if I carried on the way I was I would not complete whatever it was I had been born to do. After allowing myself to feel the sadness and think deeply about my situation, I remembered a forgotten gem of wisdom from years before. "The way through a problem is to imagine that you are on the other side of it." Suddenly, I was facing the right way, as if by magic.

CHOICES BY T.B HUMAN™

Quite some time ago I had a dream in which I found myself walking down a corridor or tunnel underground. At the time I was aware that I was dreaming, but I knew the dream was real. I seemed to be walking through a system of tunnels under the great pyramid of Cheops. The experience was profound, far more than just a dream. It was so real, the dampness of the ground filled my senses with the mustiness of old stale air, the coldness of the tunnel touched my skin and my footsteps echoed on the ancient stone floor. As I walked I could not only see the dimly lit pathway in the tunnel stretching out in front of me, but the detail of the stonework and the intricate way the light entered the chamber, in ribbons and rainbows of shafted light.

I stopped, looking upward to see where the light was coming from, and as I did I noticed that it seemed to filter down through a series of tiny vent-like structures in the ceiling high above my head. My eyes had adjusted to the dim light, so it wasn't an uncomfortable space to be in. My senses guided me as I continued along the tunnel until finally I was confronted by a solid stone wall. The wall had obviously been built to seal a tomb. "Well, what do I do now?" I asked.

A male voice answered, "Simply imagine you are on the other side of it."

Now why didn't I think of that? After all, this was a dream, and in a dream, you can do anything. Closing my dream eyes and concentrating on being on the other side of the wall was easy, and in a flash, that's exactly where I found myself.

In a moment I had somehow moved through the wall and was standing next to a large green sarcophagus. The sarcophagus was made of malachite and was carved with the love and attention that could only have been produced by a great craftsman. My hand touched the lid of the coffin, and my eyes settled upon the most beautiful face I had ever seen. As I stood looking at the coffin I knew this body had lain in state for probably thousands of years. I also knew the body lying before me was mine.

CHOICES BY T.B HUMAN™

This may sound more than a little strange, but that's exactly what happened. Ever since that day whenever life confronts me with a solid wall, all I need to do is to sit quietly and imagine myself on the other side of it, and that's what will happen. Since that day, I have had many other experiences of dreams related to that time and they always lead me through obstacles or barriers that block my growth or prevent my moving forward in this life. It is as though the wisdom of the ages is there whenever I am in need and ready to understand the knowledge.

In our daily lives, we often spend countless hours focusing on the wall, rather than imagining how it will be when we are on the other side of it. We have been taught to focus on what is wrong, rather than focus on what is right. When we focus on what is wrong, the problem just gets bigger and bigger and we can become depressed and stifled. If you allow nature to take its course, and keep your eyes, your thoughts, and your focus on where you want to go, nothing will stand in your way for long. So, when I experienced the feeling of not achieving what I came here to do, I knew I could change the outcome simply by tapping into my own center of knowing. This center of knowing would allow me to imagine how it would feel if I had accomplished defining the mysterious *It*. Once I had imagined the sense of it or the feeling of it, nature would lead me to move forward.

With all those thoughts rushing through my head I could now imagine the end of my life, in Technicolor™ and CinemaScope, with a military fanfare to boot, in this lifetime. I could see how I wanted it to be in forty years' time, and the vision was awe-inspiring. I could see the church overflowing with people and news headlines. The most powerful part of the vision for me was a photograph of me. In the photo I was a very elderly lady, seated in a study lined with books, with my children, grandchildren and great grandchildren beside me. I looked so happy and contented. The study in which I sat overlooked a beautiful hedged garden full of roses. When I looked even closer, I realized I had written a great number of those books on the shelves. Emotions overtook me, as tears streamed down my face. My heart felt as if it would break with joy, and I knew in that moment that, "Yes, I can do it." From that moment on, from that simple experience, I gained a sense of the person that I could, and would, become in this lifetime.

The little girl from the Queensland bush would make an incredible contribution to humankind and leave the world a better place for her being here. With tissues in hand, I stumbled from the bed and went to the kitchen and made a cup of tea, and then returned to the sunroom to regain my composure. What was it I had really discovered? What was it that stirred a sense of emotion that was so deep? How could I define *It* so that it could be an asset to me?

I reached for my notebook and pen and began to write the words to explain how I felt at that moment. I began to put the words together to form a small paragraph about how I would live my life from then on. Some people refer to such writing as a mission statement.

These are the words I wrote on that day:

"I want to heal my life, and in doing so, help others to have the courage to do the same. I want to help others to be able to help themselves. I want to be free of the confusion and the pain and live my life in love, not fear. I want to find out who I really am. I want to do everything I came into this life to do; I want to be able to leave this life one day with no regrets."

It was this simple statement which said it all. At the time it was my belief that this statement would be a life's work, and rightly so. There were stages when I thought I had accomplished what I had set out to do, but it was not so. I took a deep breath on each step to allow the next to appear, and life brought to me so much challenge and so much change that I hardly recognized myself when I looked back. My world would change considerably; I no longer live in the same world I did on the day I wrote that mission statement. In the intervening years thousands of people have been helped and supported to help themselves.

I am glad I did not listen to what other people said. If I had, I never would have made the necessary changes. I have learned over the years that we should never take another person's opinion of our lives seriously. Don't allow another person's perception of you to limit the person you want to become. A friend of mine once said to me, "TRUITY, you get out there and do things while others sit back and think about it, and if I told you there was something interesting at the end of the Amazon River, you would be off in your canoe and rowing." And that is true. To me anything is possible, and everything is probable. My understanding always comes, as I question what I don't know, rather than going over what I do know. The speed at which our lives evolve can only be limited by our doubts about our ability to cope. It is our doubt that creates the negative energy and the testing of our belief in ourselves along the way. I have a saying. "Let God's will be my will, and I will have the courage to keep going."

When we know what is right for us, when we no longer experience doubt, when commitment and faith meet, the heavens will move to bring you the opportunities you have been waiting for. We are all developing the courage of our convictions.

We All Came into Life to Heal Our Lives

CHOICES BY T.B HUMAN™

I have written only a little about how my life used to be. However, I am sure you can grasp the understanding that it has not been a bed of spring flowers. Now, with each passing day the memories of sadness and loneliness seem to be fading from my life. As I work out the chinks in the armor, the memories seem to be just disappearing. I don't know if this means I will cease to exist – or not. They are almost like a memory of someone else's life. As I grew into womanhood, I could not relate to the people who fought, squabbled, and were jealous and selfish around me. I didn't like the human condition very much. But sadly, in time I became just like them, feeling like I had been born into the wrong time and the wrong place.

It took many years for me to understand that the wounds we feel emotionally in the first years of our lives just keep manifesting again and again, until we finally feel the depth of the hurt and in doing so heal the wound. The aspects of my life which needed healing were simple. My family moved from a comfortable middle-class existence in England where we were surrounded by friends and family to the Queensland bush to live in a tent, with no family or support. It was a horrific blow to my psyche, for I not only lost the security of having a solid home, but I also lost my big brother who was my nurturer and protector, as he chose to stay in England and not come with us on the journey.

In those early years all I experienced was the grief and shame of poverty and the feeling that life was so hard. I honestly don't know why my mum and dad didn't pack up and return home to England. I have kept on losing homes all my life, feeling like I don't belong, because if I do I might have to face the possibility I could lose that home again, just like when I was three years old. I have continued to create poverty over and over again, until I dealt with the shame of poverty and the truth that bad things happen to good people and that other people can be ignorant and cruel.

In the beginning, the choices of life confused me greatly because every step of the way I did not know how to become the person I wanted to become. I did not have the ability to express what I was feeling; my education was limited and so was my vocabulary. My friends would say, "What is wrong with you? It's not so bad." They seemed to be able to ignore the fact they were not feeling fulfilled, a bit like ostriches with their heads in the sand. They struggled to pay their bills and fought with their husbands, constantly complained but never did anything about their situation.

This manuscript in some ways is repetitive; however, I cannot express strongly enough how I feel. Each of us has the ability to heal our lives, and not through controlling or reciting affirmations or doing anything in particular. We heal our lives when we become an honest, nonjudgmental, supportive catalyst for everyone around us. We are able to reach this state only when we learn to mentor every other human being. Life is only a struggle when we are out of step with the flow of life within us. As we reconnect with the internal flow, the natural flow, we get in step with the synchronicity, and then the opportunities come our way. The knowledge within this manuscript cannot be obtained without effort. You cannot learn by osmosis. It is not just going to happen unless you are committed to changing and growing, and you love yourself unconditionally.

CHOICES BY T.B HUMAN™

I had to learn to be true to myself, but first I needed to understand what that really involved. Each time we are not true to ourselves we suffer the consequences. In truth you cannot deny your natural nature and get off scot-free. The price for not listening to our inner knowing is often painful lessons. For some people the wake-up call comes in the form of a heart attack, a broken leg, a broken marriage, a death, or a car accident. If we don't listen, nature will always remind us to slow down and reconsider what is important. If we keep on refusing to stop and reassess life on our own accord, then ultimately nature will do it for us.

With each and every person who takes one tiny step towards healing his or her life, this planet becomes a little more balanced and healed. If everyone lived with full awareness, by his or her conscience and without fear, there would be no crime or poverty in this world. The sickness of this world is merely a manifestation of the lack of balance in people's lives. Basically, we have lost touch with our natural rhythm and ourselves. We have forgotten how to listen. Although certain energies have already been set in motion and these must run their course, we are all able to start with one tiny step.

CHOICES BY T.B HUMAN™

It is time we all got it right on the inside first. From this space we can then allow our lives to manifest in tune with our creative potential and true nature.

Each day is a new beginning; it is up to you and me what we make of it. Every person in the world has the ability to turn their life around and heal and begin to live in the now. Each of you can do just as I have done, and every answer you will ever need is within you. You have all the guidance and wisdom; all you need to do is remember how to use it.

Looking Back for the Last Time

In 1997 there was a point where, in my foolishness, I believed I had been stretched as far as anyone could be, and I fought falling into a pit of depression from which I knew there would be no return. Oh, but life was waiting to show me just how strong I am, and how resourceful one can be when pushed more than a little past the limit. At the time I had been separated from my husband for about six months, in a desperate attempt to be free and find out who I could be. He could always find ways to mentally torment the children and me; he could be downright cruel at times, to get his way.

I knew he desperately wanted me to come home, and he tried everything he could to keep the pressure on me to do so. The combination of his psychological warfare and a lack of money, combined with other, more minor problems, pushed me to a point of absolute despair. On one particular day my unhappiness overwhelmed me, and I sat sobbing in the middle of my living room floor, thinking about how I could end it all. Death seemed the only way to stop the physical, emotional and mental pain that had become my life. Yet I knew I had a choice.

It was as though I had no more strength to fight, and I knew I could not stay in the misery and unhappiness any longer. In the absolute hopelessness of my situation, I pleaded, "Why me, God? What could I have done to deserve this misery? Why me? What is it that you want from me?" Tears rolled down my face, and the pain in my heart was more than I could bear. But then the strangest feeling came over me.

CHOICES BY T.B HUMAN™

An overwhelming, inexplicable peace descended over my body, and I felt as though someone had wrapped their arms around me. I felt as much as heard a voice say, "It's all right, TRUITY. It's going to be all right; it's all right."

There is no rational explanation for the peace that descended on me that afternoon or any rational explanation for the way my life has been guided ever since. I only know my inner strength has been steadily growing, as one challenge after the other came my way. There has been a cost to the growth and change, and at times I have created situations which have been harder than anyone could ever imagine. There were also many times when my mind was filled with doubts as to whether I would make it, but I have. I now live in an entirely different world from the one faced by the confused young woman on that day.

Looking back on my life from where I stand now, there was a purpose to the struggle, for out of the experience came precious experience and knowledge. In the end I would find a better way to live life. This is what is taught through me as I mentor others to achieve their potential.

The journey from one world to another is the transition we are facing as we move into our future. Some people think we are going to be rescued by some alien fleet; others think we are going to become some enlightened beings who will live a life of constant harmony. This is all balderdash, to put it politely. The change has already begun on this earth, and it is time to create an ergo-dynamic relationship between humanity and its environment. This planet, and the life on it, is a precious gift with which we have been blessed. It is time to show the planet and other human beings respect and care. An ergo-dynamic society and environment can only manifest when the individuals in that society become aware beings, in other words, people who have run the gauntlet of the challenges of life and are spiritual people in the true sense of the word.

A spiritual person will always mentor you to improve your life and circumstances. They will lift you up, not tear you down. When we learn to listen to the silent

CHOICES BY T.B HUMAN™

beating of the heart of this world, things and life will change, and I believe that day is coming. Life really is our choice. We can keep struggling or we can let go, trust, and move forward with confidence into our future.

We have choices as to whether we stay bitter, or we forgive and forget; we have choices whether we stay lost in our thoughts or we walk outside and smell the fresh air and see the smiles on the faces of people who pass by. Life is all about choices, and as we take full responsibility for our lives and choices and realize we have the most precious gift of all, already here inside of us, we will have the ability to heal our perception of life. In doing so we will create an environment which resonates in harmony and peace while being free, free of the limits and the pain which are the result of an imbalance in our perception of the life we experience.

You see, the destiny of our planet is neither to live on some boring velvet cloud or to die through nuclear war. It is our choice to be able to experience life to the fullest, and in doing so choose how we as intelligent, responsible beings respond to the interactions we encounter. Life will never change, but how we deal with it will change, and it is moment by moment.

I now understand my life's purpose. I now understand that the reason for all I have put myself through is to help others, to show them there is a better way. It's simple, so simple that most people overlook it. In discovering myself and questioning my reality I have found a way to live a life that supports me in being a unique, creative, down-to-earth, independent, strong, gentle and feminine woman.

Finally, the fullness and freedom within is so great, there is peace and harmony, almost all the time. This fullness is not dependent upon anyone else or any belief system or religion; it comes from choosing to think about my situations from a different point of view. This knowledge does not come from books or other teachers, although you may find many other writers, teachers and healers who use the same words. The knowledge comes from my own inner knowing, which is timeless and stands clear and strong amid chaos. There really is nothing new that can be written or said. After all, we are in this life merely to remember what we already know, and ultimately everything has been experienced and encountered a million times before.

In my search for truth, life gave me the unique opportunity to experience everything I could possibly think and imagine, to grow. The ultimate goal is simply to enjoy the experience, and learn not to take it all so personally. We are here to learn the art of detached attachment, and in doing so let go of the emotional confusion which is generated by our unhealed perceptions of life. This is the art of letting go of the ownership of others and outcomes and being individuals with an individual role to play, the art of taking responsibility for ourselves, while joining with others to create new life. Somehow, then, one plus one really does equal three. We each walk alone; however, when we join our hearts, a third identity is created.

We must learn not to take this experience we call human life too seriously. Life is about manifesting experiences. The more we stand in our truth, the more our lives will change, as circumstances around us rearrange to the align with our truth. Whatever is false in your life must crumble and fall away. Only experiences which are truly aligned with your life and your purpose will remain. Our body's energy attracts to it what it already has. If we have chaos inside us from our hidden insecurities, we will manifest those energies into real-life experiences in order to work though the limits of our fears. When we are clear and strong in thought, the thought must manifest as a physical reality sooner or later. But remember, even a mighty oak takes time to grow; it does not appear instantly overnight.

The Aloneness

I used to be lonely all the time; now I choose to be alone, most of the time. In that aloneness I am no longer lonely; I am at peace. I never thought I would travel so far and learn so much, to be still, so alone. It somehow seems a little strange for me to feel this way; after all, the journey to heal my life was instigated in the beginning in an attempt to find a life in which I would no longer be alone! The understanding and knowledge I have gathered enables me to realize there are precious few who can understand my reality, for precious few have ever experienced it. It's 1997 and my New Year's Day has been crammed packed with astounding realizations. I seem to feel this way at the beginning of each new year when I look back at the changes that have occurred. During all those past years I never dreamed I was just like everyone else. I am the same as you and the same as the Queen of England and the same as the street kid who sleeps in the park. I am exactly the same as everyone who has ever felt alone. We all think we are in the minority but in fact we are the majority.

As my journey into self-healing began, I was blessed by occasionally finding a companion in spirit, a fellow traveler who was also on their journey. There were even times when I was lucky enough for them to be able to stay for a while, touching my life, and encouraging me to believe I wasn't the only one out there after all. These precious moments of understanding and communication with another gave me the sense of being home, gave me strength during those times when it all just got too hard. Each time I started to become comfortable with my life, though, things would change, and the comfort would soon be gone. The sense of being safe and at home was as elusive as the mist moving across the water on a winter's day. One moment I would feel, "Yes, I've got it," and then it would be gone, and I would sink into the feeling of not being able to see tomorrow.

Being a spiritual person has nothing to do with being psychic; it is simply living each day of your life being true to yourself, never creating intentional harm to another person, and striving to become a better person by developing your untapped potential.

Turn It Around

Because of our perception of life, most of us spend the larger part of our lives searching for something. The strange thing is that often the thing we search for we already have, but can't see. One of the grandest illusions and distractions of all is that we have to search for anything. Everything you need, all the knowledge of all times, is within you. All you need to do is allow yourself to remember what you already know. We are all searching to get back into step with the rhythm of life, and we can do this by simply learning to stop thinking so much.

We can do this by remembering how to meditate or sit with our own thoughts, and allow ourselves to have a little peace and quiet each day. Being constantly busy, and having a mind that is full of chatter all the time, is a major symptom of our lives and energy being out of balance.

The Search for Buried Treasure

If I were to give you a map and guarantee you would find the greatest treasure you could ever imagine, would you take the chance? This is what I am offering you right this moment. Within you is a storehouse of the most precious gems that have ever been seen in this world. And you don't need to become a workshop junkie to find them. You don't even need me. Isn't that wonderful? All you need is within you. I know I keep saying the same thing over and over. Do you have the courage to change; are you willing to take responsibility for your life? Your life is the direct result of your thoughts.

The moment you have the courage to take responsibility for your life you are well on your way to finding the treasure. The storehouse for the treasure is so obvious most people overlook it. They use the wrong instruments to try to find it; they use the active mind and rehash old logic. They use all manner of means of control, but still it eludes them. But with courage and responsibility as your tools, you will have the strength to be open to listen to truth. Not the words other people lay on you, those emotional, manipulative tools people use in order to get you to behave the way they want you to, because you feel guilty or want to please them. What I am talking about is the voice of wisdom that echoes deep within you. You remember it: surely you do. Let me remind you.

Do you remember when you were about twelve years old and you stole those twenty cents from your mother or father's wallet? Do you remember how you felt? Remember the uneasy feeling in your stomach. That feeling is your marker for direction that is your wisdom talking to you. Sometimes it may even be yelling at you, but mostly you try not to listen. It is your choice whether you listen to it or not, but when you don't listen you can just bet you're headed up a pathway that will teach you some very important and often painful lessons.

Now that you remember what your conscience is like, it will be easy for a while for you to feel it again, won't it? You have found the first gem, and now if you're brave you can keep reading and find the next clue. To make it a little bit of a challenge to you I have hidden the rest of the gems in the chapters that follow. See if you can find them all.

Free at Last

The hardest of all lessons for me to learn was to be a free soul. That freedom comes from not needing to feel anguish over what I do or do not have. How much stress is created in your life through what you would like to have? Right at this moment, do you have what you need to be alive and well?

Now I find I am more discerning, and I avoid spending time with people who are manipulative and need to control their environment. I do not choose to live in that energy. When I am with these people I often feel like a strong-headed filly being rounded up by the farmer's dog. I simply jump the fences and head off to another pasture where I can be myself and live in the truth that my own sense of knowing brings to me. Today I tend to go with the flow; I no longer want or need to control my environment to feel safe and secure. Do you go with the flow in your life?

Do you know it is not possible for you to be in the wrong place at the wrong time?

Wherever you are, whatever you experience, it is for you to make some sort of realization about yourself and your life.

CHOICES BY T.B HUMAN™

It's All a Matter of Perception

During my years of working with people, I have been amazed by the way some people think. While working in Sydney I met a lady called Vera. Vera was a young and attractive, well educated woman who had just separated from her husband of twenty- five years. When I met her for the first appointment, she was distraught. Vera had been separated for a year and was living in her apartment looking out over Central Park in Sydney. Vera was distraught because she was worried about her future. She was terrified she would not have enough money to last her the rest of her life. At the time, Vera was working in a take-out chicken shop. She was forty-five at the time, and her husband had custody of their children, so she had no dependents to take care of. I talked with her for a while and she told me she owned the luxury apartment she lived in, was driving a new BMW, and to top it off her husband's divorce settlement was four-and-a-half million dollars. She was upset because he had at least twenty-five million dollars in the bank.

How ironic, I thought. I had just come out of a twenty-five-year marriage with only three thousand dollars, and all of that had been taken up in legal expenses. I had nowhere to live and nothing to fall back on except my belief in myself. The contrast left me shaking my head. I was absolutely amazed by the whole situation. You see, life really is a matter of perception. What is terrible for one person is beyond belief to another. Over the years, I have learned abundance is a state of mind, not a state of pocket.

Whenever the ego is involved, a person will continually attempt to guarantee safety and security by locking up and controlling their movements. Without even realizing how they are restricting their lives, their need for security will restrict their ability to manifest a wonderful, expanding potential future. Life is certainly an amazing evolutionary experience, and mine was about to move forward once again full throttle. My own learning curve was about to be accentuated once more.

The concept of *TRUITY Choices* was being born. By the time I moved to Brisbane with the family I was fully ensconced in developing the early prototype for the first product of TRUITY. I had quit my job and decided to go whole hog and go for it and design the product, write the product content, and conduct the trials for the product. This was long before I began to understand and become adept with aspects of identity branding, patents and trademarks, and other legal terms, as well as developing a marketing plan and strategy. When I had a moment to breathe, I was worrying about where the money was going to come from.

Did It to Myself Again

In the late nineteen nineties, my health was failing once again. I had not given myself time to recover fully from my bout with glandular fever, and I had been working too many hours with too little resources to fall back upon. When you add to the ingredients of the cocktail a bad relationship with a gentleman called JP and my determined personality trait of "Don't tell me I can't," the whole project became a bit much for one person. Lynne rolled up her sleeves and joined me in the battle to succeed to bring to the world the concept of TRUITY.

CHOICES BY T.B HUMAN™

Throughout the days of life at Number 62, the family home, Lynne stood by me as a friend and confidant, encouraging me when I became disheartened, taking care of me when I could not get out of bed because of my illness. Our friendship is one which has overcome many obstacles and challenges, including the fact that we drive each other nuts at times. To our amusement, once or twice we have even been accused of being a gay couple. A confused jealous male friend of mine could never understand that Lynne and I were so aligned to the same mission and that was why we got along so well. He tried hard to dislodge Lynne from the process of the development of TRUITY, yet today she is still the one doing the hard yards, and he like so many others, is nowhere to be found.

It's a sad thing that life has come to the point where two women or two men cannot be seen as close friends, without people thinking there has to be more to it. But that is probably a sign of the times we live in, and how sick society is in general and why we need products like *TRUITY Choices*.

CHOICES BY T.B HUMAN™

I know the earlier chapters of this book go to depths of the difficult times I have encountered. However, it's important to understand that when a person goes through so many hard times, eventually something changes inside, and that person begins to make light and see the funny side in everything. There have been so many moments of devastation and despair, and they can only be balanced by our ability to turn the moments into moments of black humor. Today I seem to laugh at most things. No point in years has brought the self-examination and self-honesty that would strip you to the bare bones, or times so sad and heartbreaking that friends leave rather than be exposed to the depth of soul commitment I have for my vision and the good that I know can be done through applying TRUITY.

For years, I have lived breathed and slept TRUITY; I have had to selfishly stay singular in my focus and hell-bent on getting this giant child of peace to its place of birth, believing all the while that the sun will one-day dance again, and there will be life for me besides TRUITY. When I met Lynne, instantly we knew we shared a bond that went far beyond this lifetime. A friendship so strong and enduring that neither time nor circumstances could undo the commitment we both have to doing what we do.

We both also knew there is a third person out there somewhere in the wings, waiting to join us to finish what we began centuries ago. We have managed to cull the prospective people down to a handful, and yet we cannot preempt the connection. It is for him or her to do that, when that person is ready. Destiny is destiny, and what is meant to be will be, and we know this as sure as the sun rises in the sky each morning. So, we wait, impatiently at times, but we wait.

Blocked or Not Blocked?

During the last two days I have had three phone calls from clients / friends who have all been feeling desperate because they feel that their lives were not flowing. For some strange reason we have a habit of thinking that whenever life is not moving ahead swiftly, we must be blocked. So-called spiritual people will feed us false teachings and beliefs that past-life energy blocks us, or our guides are blocking us, and / or our lack of knowledge is blocking our progression. Such false teachings have the potential to disempower our lives and energy.

It has been only during the last few years that I have truly begun to understand we are never blocked, ever. I had an interesting conversation with my oldest daughter when she phoned me a few days ago. "Mum, what am I doing wrong?" were her first words. "I can't seem to be able to do the things that Beverly and Barb can do," she went on. "Beverly keeps telling me there is this entity or spirit around me who is blocking me from developing and I am holding myself back." She was almost in tears, and I could hear the frustration in her voice as she tried to maintain her composure.

My immediate response to the statement was, "That's garbage," and the words just tumbled out of my mouth without my even thinking. "Did you know it might not be in your best interest to develop those skills? Did you ever stop to think that if you did, it might take you on a detour in life you are not meant to experience at this time?" I took a deep breath and continued. "I know that often to the unaware it seems like we are blocked, when it is, in fact, the greatest gift which our higher consciousness can give us. There were many times when I felt just like you do now, frustrated and confused because I didn't know how to understand everything.

"Looking back now I realize just how much help I had in staying on track. My path in life has been guided and protected, not blocked, and yours is the same." By the end of our conversation she had begun to realize her helpers in spirit were making sure that she was in the right place at the right time, and the doors to learning different skills and understandings only open when the mind is strong enough to cope.

Each of us has a divine plan, a life path to follow. We often have a terrible aversion to being in any space where nothing happens. That blocked feeling which accompanies the void is just a waiting place. I remember hearing the saying, "When the fishermen can't go out to sea they mend their nets," and this is true for all of us. We are often given precious times when we are meant to rest and build our energy.

CHOICES BY T.B HUMAN™

However, most of us struggle, complain, thrash about and never allow ourselves the time to just sit and know that everything is all right.

During the last year I have spent a great deal of time sitting and watching the sea and an enormous amount of time sleeping. Those around me could not understand why I was not panic-stricken as my savings dwindled and I did not look for work or clients. Everyone was so used to seeing me acting like superwoman. To see me quietly resting was quite a turnabout. I was worn out and needed to rest, so I simply made a healing space of how things were, and thank God, I did. I know it is only a few short days before that luxury of time, space and sunshine will soon to be transformed into jet planes and suitcases, and that is fine.

The blessing I have experienced during the last year wasn't having money in the bank or someone to share my time with. The blessing was I had the space and the opportunity to change my attitude despite what was being forced upon me by the universe, and make it an advantage to me. It seems funny when I think of how I spent many days pretending I was on holiday, just so I would not stress out. I used to smile to myself as I walked along the headland and watched the tourists trying to cram all the healing and relaxation into a week or two. Thoughts used to run through my mind. "Thank you, God, for the space, and thank you for the grace, and, yes, I do know that this quiet time, too, will pass."

Fun and Games at Number 62

When I moved into Number 62, my sister M lived there, and her thirty-year-old daughter V came and went at regular intervals. Mum lived in the flat downstairs. My eldest brother V owned the house; he had bought it as a family base, so mum would not have to worry about paying rent or having someone keep an eye on her safety as she grew older. It was a lovely home with a beautiful landscaped garden. The house was more than big enough for all of us, and so with permission from Big Brother, I took up residence in the front room. It was here that life would hand me some of its master challenges to face. I had begun the development of product, and energy and money were being chewed up at an incredible rate.

Not having business support that I could rely upon was one thing that hampered my progress during that time. I found not even money could buy much needed advice from so-called experts, people who were supposed to know how to develop a new product and invention. The problem was, I could not get them to understand fully the concept, so I battled with people wanting to put their own connotations upon everything I tried to achieve.

It was like trying to pour a watermelon through a funnel. The cost was financial, physical and emotional. It cost me a lot of money in the long run to learn that I was the only one who could do this. My lesson was to trust my own judgment. I looked to gain the support of people I admired and wrote letters to everyone I could think of to try to gain some advice, support or encouragement.

Even though many replied, no one would give me the time of day. My naive belief, that people who had made it against the odds would care, was to be shattered time and time again, as no one offered to guide me or help me despite my persistent requests for help. I suppose they just thought like many other people that I was some nutty woman with a vision and of little importance to the scheme of things. So, I just kept on keeping on, acting with precision, trusting in God and my knowing to show me the way. I just kept taking one step at a time forward into the unknown without a parachute.

The universe was not happy with hurling just business challenges at me. No, not on your life. My health was disintegrating before my eyes, with doctors unable to accurately pinpoint what on earth was going on. I kept hearing a creaking noise in my head when I lay to sleep at night, like tree roots growing, is how I described it to the doctors at the time. They looked at me as though I were mad and said, "We can find nothing wrong with you." The stress and the strain were about to take their biggest toll of all. On 30th August 1997 I suffered a brain bleed, or a small stroke, which was compounded by glandular fever, and the result was I was totally unable to take care of myself. The bizarre thing is my family thought I was putting it on, for attention. I was so ill, I just wanted to go to sleep and never wake up again. I was too tired to argue or plead my case; I just stayed in my room and slept for days and days, and little by little tried to put my life back together, step by painful step.

When I moved home, the major challenge was a combination of the facts that my health and Mum's health were both disintegrating fast. With Mum it was to be expected, for after all, she was now in her eighties and had not been well for a very long time. I was financially in a difficult situation, with no income at all, so pride had to take the back seat. With cap in hand, health shattered in a million pieces, I set up my bedroom at the house to double as office, lounge and bedroom. Luckily it was an enormous room. It had softly colored pink walls and old-fashioned ten-foot ceilings. Luckily, the room was big enough for my desk, computer, table and chairs and bed.

I knew Mum was hanging on to make sure I was all right. However, I also knew that her body was failing fast, and no matter how stubborn and strong-minded she was, it was only a matter of time. Finally, on 19th June 1998 Mum passed away, leaving the family to deal with its grief and send her ashes to rest back in England with the rest of the family, tucked away next to Dad, Grandma, and my brother and sister in the family grave. Those days in Number 62 can probably go down in history as some of the most challenging and the most difficult of days in the story of TRUITY and its creation, and yet little did I know the worst was yet to come.

The lack of vision by those around me was a constant challenge, especially combined with my poor health and the fact I had no money. I still could not let go of my vision to create this tool that would help others live a better life. I still didn't have the strength or endurance to be able to go out to work, so there was no money. All I had was a stubborn will and the vision of what I wanted to accomplish.

I had to find a way to have the first TRUITY products developed and manufactured. I knew what it could do to help people and I also knew that it was not going to be an easy task. After all, who would give a girl from the bush with no business credibility a go?

Where would I raise the money to keep going? I had estimated it would cost about five hundred thousand dollars to get the first product up and out there, and if I had stopped at the first product that would have probably been quite enough. However, building a brand took a little more. At the time I probably would never have forged ahead if I had realized what it would cost me in energy, commitment and money. In fact, I never dreamed it would in fact take a million dollars, plus five more years of constantly driving myself beyond the limits of endurance, and at times sanity, to reach the point of marketing the product, let alone the final goal.

The major deterrent to my achieving my goal was the fact I did not trust my own judgment. Being new in the corporate world, I was encouraged by everyone to take another person's advice. I will never do that again, at least not in the same way, Other people's advice turned out to be almost the undoing of me and very close to the destruction of my life's work and the end of TRUITY. I had unwisely listened to the advice of a so-called expert and called the product TRUITY instead of *Choices*. TRUITY was my brand, not the product name, and somehow those around me could not understand where I was taking the whole project and insisted that TRUITY be it. The problems arose, as there was no public association with TRUITY and what it did, and we didn't have the money to promote it or achieve the outcome in its current form.

I want to point out here that anyone ever trying to do something like this should make sure they have the emotional support to do the hard yards. I did not; I did, however, have a strong spiritual sense of connectedness and guidance, which have keep me aware of how to deal with situations that otherwise I would have found absolutely impossible.

The Eternal Questions

What am I here for?
Who am I?
What is it I am trying to prove here?

CHOICES BY T.B HUMAN™

Over the last months my day-to-day life often seemed to be entirely taken up with trying to reach something that is somewhere out there. Everyone out there in the New Age world seemed to be searching for *It*, too! What was even more perplexing being that I hadn't yet found anyone who had found *It*. Yet everyone wanted to reach *It*. I couldn't quite figure it out. How had I stepped onto this roller coaster? Did I really want fame and fortune? Did I really think I had to change my life to be able to experience *It*?

I know many of the people around me believe when they become successful the internal recurring restlessness will magically disappear, their lives will be transformed, and they will live happily ever after. With this belief firmly entrenched in the back of their minds, they are often more than willing to sacrifice the irreplaceable moments and simple pleasures of today. I hated to admit it, but I found myself wanting the life I had had before. I wanted the security of a marriage and family, and I missed being a mum.

CHOICES BY T.B HUMAN™

One of my favorite songs on the CD by Jennifer Warnes called *Famous Blue Raincoat.* is "I Came So Far for Beauty." The song tells the story of a woman who was searching for *It*. She gave up her family, changed her clothes to black, changed everything in her life to look for the elusive, only to find at the end of her life that she had left the most precious things unfinished. She had not been a mother to her children or a lover to her husband, and life was now filled with nothing but sadness and regrets.

It is a wonderful song and applicable to so many who are now on the search to find the elusive It. Don't throw away what you have while looking for something better. Usually what you have is perfect; you just need to relax and begin to respect and enjoy each other, and life will do the rest. In hindsight, I know now that my life with my ex-husband was a good life. It's just we didn't communicate very well. I had what I wanted; it was just I didn't know I had it because it had been there for so long. It was all I knew, but was everything I could not see.

Don't Pull the Wings off the Butterfly

Today in 2003, I am still a single woman – by choice. I have had more marriage proposals than most women could imagine, but at the end of the day men either find my dedication to my path too challenging, or I don't find them open-minded enough to let me be me. Besides that, I don't want to deal with all the crap they are still hanging on to. I have been surprised at how many men would like to pull the wings off the butterfly, or maybe I have just not yet met the man who is my match. As Robert would say, "God help the man who tries to tell you what to do. You're nobody's doormat." Back in 1996 I didn't have a clue how I was going to get TRUITY off the ground, and men, well, I just didn't have time or the energy for commitment at that point anyway. There have been a few wonderful experiences along the way; I am human after all. But there is something inside me which yearns for someone who I have not yet met.

He comes to me in dreams and is always present, but just out of reach. One day, he will come home, of that I have no doubt. My love life could fill several books with wisdom and insight. I have no regrets, only good thoughts for those who have shared my life. Be it for a week or a year, I thank them. To this day, my vision leads me onward. It gives me the strength to stand strong when conflict reigns around me. My faith in the goodness of what I have developed won't allow me to let go of the project, no matter how much pain and suffering I am faced with.

I have the belief that one day it will all work out and fall into place, that there is a need and a place for my TRUITY in this world. Heaven help anyone who stands in my way, and heaven's blessings on those who have held me up when I was weak and tired. It was to be months and, in fact, years before I realized that the extent of the energy and effort I had put out there was far beyond what any sane person would have attempted. You see, I didn't know what I didn't know, so boundaries that would have stopped others in their tracks I simply found a way to overcome. To me nothing was impossible. I was committed to the vision of reaching my goal, and no one or anything was going to stop me. I prayed a great deal, and miracle after miracle occurred.

CHOICES BY T.B HUMAN™

I turned every obstacle into an opportunity and never stayed down or depressed for more than the time it was appropriate. I bounce back incredibly fast, thank God. Frustrations reached an all-time high in 1998 when my family, that is, my brothers and sister thought I had gone completely nuts. I was hell-bent on doing this thing called TRUITY, and one of my brothers, Paul, was even convinced I needed psychiatric help for depression, and my other brother made comments like, "When are you going out to get a real job?"

My frustrations flared, and I retaliated with, "I'm not sick because I'm depressed, I'm depressed because I'm so bloody sick. My body hurts, and I have no energy and I am sick and tired of the doctors and the constant stream of tests. Can't anyone understand that? It's simple. I can see the words on my gravestone, 'I told you I was sick.'"

No matter how hard I tried, no one seemed to comprehend that I was seriously ill. They were all too busy with not coping with my situation. My children were all busy with their own children, partners and lives, and feeling the loss of a mother who was so preoccupied with this thing she called TRUITY that they couldn't understand that the relationships were more than a little stretched at times. Looking back, I seemed to be the only one who could see the vision of what I was about to give birth to, and that is probably quite normal in the circumstances. That was, until I met my trusty buddy, Lynne, and she volunteered to join in and be a part of this classic adventure. Before moving home, I had managed to complete the first draft of TRUITY.

The content had all been written, the design roughly made, even the first trial games held. I had even been moved to meet the need, as bold as to have the first viability study conducted and the first of the patents and trademarks lodged. Every cent of my money had been devoured in the process, and the challenge became making a penny go around ten times before I spent it once. I forged ahead with the belief that when commitment and effort met, heaven and earth would shift and give me a means to keep going.

CHOICES BY T.B HUMAN™

Hang On; Help Is on Its Way

23rd March 1999. I was once again trying to contact Deepak and Wayne, and once again I was designing new brochures and trying in my mind to begin to have a cohesive description of what it is that TRUITY does. I have found the task not nearly as easy as one might first think. Wayne had written several encouraging notes, but nothing substantial had come of the contact.

My diary notes around this time read, "I am having a very hard time at the moment. once again questioning everything. I don't see how I am possibly going to make it though this one. For the first time my faith is more than a bit shaky. It's hard to trust and let things fall into place, although I keep hearing the words, "In God we trust." That's on the American dollar, isn't it?

I kept hitting brick walls with the people I tried to contact. I always thought that people would see the vision I have and want to help. How naive I was. I wrote letters, emailed, sent games, did everything possible to raise someone's curiosity. I targeted people

CHOICES BY T.B HUMAN™

like B, Chopra, Suzuki, McLain, Robbins, Clinton, people who I thought had a bit of insight and dedication to make this planet a better place, all people who knew what it was like to struggle to create something better of this world. But no help came; no one was interested in some woman from Australia with a vision and a plan. I tried not to feel sorry for myself, but at times it did get a bit disheartening, and sometimes it's even harder to keep going when there is nothing solid coming back.

I supposed to some extent I lived in another world in those days. My dreams became the guiding keys into each day. I wrote them down and waited to see at the end of the day what made sense and what was just irrelevant jumble. Little by little, I learned the language of my own psyche, and how my unconscious could communicate with my conscious mind. In hindsight, I have no doubt that the capacity of the mind to cross physical barriers is far greater than we ever could dream. I knew that with a little attention I could keep myself informed about events and people anywhere, any time. I suppose this is how the seers and the holy men used their abilities in centuries past. My dreams were to become a source of insight greater than I could have ever comprehended possible. I still wonder sometimes if being profoundly intuitive is a gift or a curse. From where I am today, I surely could not imagine living life without such acute sensory perception. To give the reader an insight into how exact my intuition can be, I have included an excerpt from my diary.

9th June 1999. I dreamt I was sailing off on a boat with that tall blonde man. In the dream I was trying to catch eels. Slippery little fellows, there were tons of them and they were all beautiful, covered in spots, and slippery. Also in the dream, M, my sister, was angry with me because I owed her sixty-nine dollars. Then the power bill came today, and it was exactly sixty-nine dollars each when shared among the three of us. M was as angry as hell that the bill was so high. In the same dream, I also dreamt that a big black spider bit me on the neck, and I woke up panicking and not able to breathe. Later that morning my daughter phoned me to tell me that my son had been bitten by something on the neck and was quite ill, and having trouble breathing.

After many years of watching my dreams I am able to draw insight, warning and knowing of what is happening around me and to my life. It's quite uncanny, really. Over the years it has saved me from many a disaster and let me know when something is wrong with my children, even when I am on the other side of the world.

Going Electronic

One of the challenges I would face was learning about the Internet and web design. I was a novice in every sense of the word regarding the process of having websites registered and e-commerce attached, and found it all totally overwhelming, to say the least. At first, I was terrified I would blow up the computer, and I had no idea how the whole thing worked or how one ever got to the final product of a web page. John C, a friend of a friend, came to the rescue and began little by little educating me in the ways of the electronic world. Now, years later, it all seems light years ago, as I write the web pages and develop marketing tools to be used in getting my work out to the world. Yes, I have had to grow, and yes, it has hurt like hell, but yes, it has been worth it.

The change to thinking of company development via satellite technology and Internet development was going to happen easily. However, we were about to experience some very expensive and painful lessons. Common problems with developing anything new, as I have mentioned before, is that you get tons of experts, who all just want to do it their way. Generally, for us, the result turned out to be an expensive learning curve. Thousands of dollars were charged for products which really did not do justice to what we were attempting to achieve. In the end, I have learned to find consultants who are willing to allow you to work alongside them, so the end product will be aligned with the original concept with very little time wasted and saving tons of money.

18th June 1999. Today I received a letter from Oprah. She said she is too busy. Ah well, I will write back again. Someone has to open a door for me soon, or will I have to kick one in? Lynne and I have been spending time searching out the celebrities who we one day want to have involved in our charity work. We thought if we could get some good PR or if we could possibly get their endorsement, it would be worth gold. If we failed on the first option then in five to ten years when things have moved to a position where we are known, we won't have any trouble getting them on our side. Or at least that was the plan. And so, life went on. As usual things never did work out the way I thought they would at the time. It seemed as if God had other plans. The priorities seemed to require that I do some serious work on healing my relationships with my children and at the same time get healthy and finish the project to the final stage where it could be launched. The lessons of 1999–2001 were ones never to be forgotten, and ultimately would be the pain and challenge which would give me the clarity and strength to keep on keeping on.

Conflict of Interest

I found, as days flowed into months, I had a fight developing inside of me. There was a growing conflict of interest. I knew it was impossible for things to keep flowing if I could not find an answer to this dilemma. My peace was leaving me. I had to find a way to stop the battle and get back on track.

If there is conflict, wealth may be gained, but it will be short-lived. I was about to experience the full confrontation of the conflict, which lay hidden inside of me. One way or the other, the conflict had to end, and peace had to once again fill my life. I had to find away to forgive myself for the past and let go of feeling guilty about how things had been. I seemed to find plenty of people who wanted a relationship with me, but for me they were not "the one," something wasn't right. I was wise enough to know that the world reflects our inner energy. Things we push away can come to us through others. Anger if denied will often come as violence from another. It's only when we accept all our qualities and then harness them as our allies that we flourish.

I knew that there is a common link between what we achieve and what we believe. My problem was that more than anything I wanted the acknowledgement, love, and acceptance of those around me. I started to overreact because I felt no one understood what I had set out to achieve. I was scared to death of failure, and that fear was inevitably drawing failure closer with every breath I took.

The subtle energies were guiding me, swinging me back and forth as I looked for clarity. I was losing myself, becoming this other person, this so-called businesswoman, distanced from people and the very core of what made me essentially who I was. I sought to find clarity, but all that followed was a hollow emptiness that robbed everyone around me of the love that had started the whole journey. I was lost, and I didn't even know it.

Without knowing it, I had created a false personality, one that was not connected to the person who I truly am. I had cut off the depth of love, cut away the preciousness of allowing people to get close to me. My creativity had taken over, and I was, without realizing it, controlling my life by proxy. I tried harder and harder to be the businesswoman that my advisers told me I had to be. I changed my direction, followed their advice, all the while getting further and further away from the core of my energy, and the core of what TRUITY stood for.

I was fighting with myself. That was obvious. No matter what I tried to achieve, it didn't work, my timing was out, my employees were making mistakes that were beyond comprehension, and my life was in tatters. My business was failing, all because I let others lead me, all because I took their advice over my own gut intuition.

I had to make some hard decisions, and so I made them. I was going home. I was going back to face my ex-husband and my children, and I was determined to heal my relationships with my family and friends and above all "to get a life."

Home Again

June 2002. What am I doing back here? Funny thing is, I didn't fit here when I lived here before. What on earth makes me think I will fit in now? The Brisbane offices of TRUITY International are now closed. Sometimes I wonder if it ever happened at all. My staff let me down; I feel used and abused, and there are so many unanswered questions. I sit and watch the passing parade of faces, quite surprised that I can still recognize so many of the people as they pass by where I sit.

My thoughts race, and it astounds me that in ten years, the same people are still here looking exactly as they did, doing exactly the same things. How bizarre. For a moment, I feel like I must be caught in a time warp. It's like nothing has changed but me. I take another sip of my hot chocolate and wonder at it all. The marshmallow in the chocolate makes it sweet and sticky as it warms my body with forbidden and almost sinful pleasure.

My thoughts turn back to the passing parade. Trying not to look too obvious, I find myself searching the faces of the passersby, for signs of the slightest glimmer of recognition. No, not a flash of recognition anywhere. Eyes meet and not an ounce of acknowledgement or a flicker of a memory shows. Quite astounding, I think to myself. Through the archway strides a tall, thin man carrying a half a dozen shopping bags. He continues to move directly towards me. I smile, recognizing him immediately, and yet it's as though I am invisible! Without a second look, he simply continues his journey.

Fifteen years ago, I served him his beer every night after work. He knew my husband and my family, and yet our eyes meet, and he passes by without so much as a second look. I pinch myself, to see if I am here, shaking my head in disbelief. The question running once again through my mind is, "Could I have I changed that much?"

The next person to catch my eye is Sharon. Sharon and I used to pick blueberries together in the freezing cold for months on end, year after year. Even she doesn't show any sign of recognition towards me; her eyes meet mine, and nothing happens, no sign of seeing me. For the next hour, face after face passes by in the parade of life without a sign of any recognition from anyone. As I sit here, I remember a quote from Nelson Mandela's book, *A Long Walk to Freedom*. "There is nothing like returning to a place that remains unchanged to find the ways in which you yourself have altered." Well, isn't that the truth.

My thoughts begin to race. Have I changed that much? I know it's been a while, but it's not as if I have never come back before. Puzzled, I sit almost hypnotized by the situation I find myself in. I have come home, and yet it's like I am a perfect stranger. "What am I doing here?" The city was an education, that's for sure. I somehow thought coming home would help me begin to rebuild some sort of a life, or finish unfinished business. What do I do now? Do I contact old friends? Do I make new friends? Do I want anyone here to know me, or do I simply want a space where I can blend into the background and not be recognized at all by anyone? Do I want to just be? So many thoughts and questions, and yet I know with every part of me that this is where I am meant to be. How strange this all feels, kind of surreal. Out of the corner of my eye I catch sight of a tiny gray-haired old lady with a profoundly hunched back, pushing her walking frame across the room towards one of the shops. It must be pension day, seems to be a lot of elderly folk out today.

CHOICES BY T.B HUMAN™

The old lady struggles forward, proudly taking one step at a time, gasping for breath and leaning her tiny body against the frame on the walker for support. My head spins and my mind whirls and just for a moment, it's ten years earlier. For a moment, I am back in time and I am sitting in the same donut shop with my cup of tea, watching and waiting for Mum to push her walker, shuffling her way across to where I sit, stopping every few feet to catch her breath. I sit patiently waiting for Mum to reach my table to join me, and I dare not rush from my seat to help her, as I know only too well what her independence means to her. Just at that moment, the elderly lady notices my gaze, and stops, smiling back at me. Tears fill my eyes and I realize Mum is gone and how much I miss her.

Somewhere behind me someone drops a metal tray, and my attention is brought sharply back to the weight of the cup in my hands. I am glad of being pulled back from that space of missing Mum. It hurts, and I don't like to feel the loss, as it is still so fresh in my memory and painful to deal with. I change my focus, yummy hot chocolate, but it's nearly all gone. It tasted really good. I wrap both of my hands around the cup to absorb every ounce of warmth from its smooth white surface. Little piles of powdered chocolate are stuck to the rim of the cup, and I dab at the fine brown powder with my tongue. Not very ladylike, I must admit, but I sure enjoyed every ounce of the sweetness.

The morning had an eerie sense of time warp as I sat amongst that crowd of people in the middle of the shopping mall. I could have been a visitor from another planet for all anyone cared, or beamed in from another place or time, but at that moment, it did not feel like how I imagined coming home should feel.

When I purchased my hot chocolate, I had purposely chosen a seat facing the double electronic doors of the shopping center. I always have been a people watcher, but today is more like a quest, I suppose. I have been here for about half an hour at least and it's almost become a game now. How long will it take for someone to recognize me?

I'm not sure what I am waiting for. I just feel compelled to watch and to wait. No sooner had I thought that thought than, as if by magic, there through the door appeared a friendly face. "My God, he has not changed an ounce; I didn't know he was back here, too." Without thinking, I rush to my feet, leaving my bags of goodies spread all over the table with the now nearly empty mug of hot chocolate. I push back my chair and find myself rushing forward, calling out, "Robert, Robert, it's so good to see you."

I can laugh about it now, but the poor man was quite taken aback at the time, even to the extent that he stopped in midstride and took a step or two backwards. For a moment, Robert's face looked puzzled, and he searched my eyes for the connection. You could hear his unspoken words, "Who on earth was this woman?" Then a flood of recognition showed as a smile spread across his face. "TRUITY?" he said in his still broad American drawl, "Is that really you? My goodness, you have changed so much. You're so feminine."

It was a comment I wasn't sure quite how to take at the time. Without thinking, my arms went full circle around his neck and I planted a very enthusiastic kiss on his cheek almost overwhelming the poor fellow. Robert always was a very shy guy, gentle in ways and gentle by nature, and not one to openly show the world the depth of his presence. "Want to join me for a coffee?" I asked, and before he had time to answer, "Come on and sit with me for a minute or two and tell me what you have been doing with yourself all these years." That's one thing about good friends, you may not see them for years and years, and then you pick up right where you left off. The last time Robert and I had spoken was back in 1993, just before my third trip to the States.

"Where do I begin?" was my response to Robert's question.

"What on earth have you been up to," he asked. "Where have you been? You look so different, I wouldn't have recognized you." And in that moment, I knew what I had been sitting in the mall waiting for, another old friend, and another companion in spirit to rejoin me on the journey.

"Robert," I paused, unsure if he was ready for this tale. "The last ten years have been like a long walk, or should I say crawl, over broken glass, through fire and freezing blizzards, with moments of intense heartache that would in a moment be transformed by sunshine that was blinding with its beauty." I paused for a moment. "Not only that, I have been on an adventure that has taken me to a place where everything within me that was not truth was just stripped away.

"I suppose you could say I have been on my own journey to the outer limits of my body, mind, and soul's endurance, and found my Holy Grail." I leaned back on the metal chair, and watched his reaction to my statement.

Shaking his head with wonder and disbelief he answered, "Well, with the changes I can see and feel in you, I don't doubt that for one minute." He leaned forward inquisitively.

I looked down at my cup and swirled the last of the liquid around and around, stirring the chocolate up into the last of the warm milk as I spoke. I could feel my eyes glaze over as my inner vision took over. I pulled upon the vivid memories, recalling scene after scene from the last years. "In fact, the last years have been all of that and more."

I paused once again, sipping the warm, sweet liquid from the cup. "I have been around the world to faraway places. I found myself caught up in things no sane person would have dared to get involved in." Without being conscious of my actions, my eyes scanned the room as I continued to speak. "At one time, I found myself involved with a man who worked for military intelligence, and the result of that was I was put under surveillance. I have been spied upon, threatened, had my mail disappear for months on end, had my phone tapped, and that was just for starters." I was now smiling to myself at the ridiculousness of what had happened, and taking a long deep breath, I continued. "And all the while all this was going on, I had to stretch my business acumen beyond sanity, and become corporate and credible. The shy girl from the bush had to find a way to be right out there, strong and accurate."

CHOICES BY T.B HUMAN™

Robert sat looking at me with his mouth slightly ajar, as though he was halfway through speaking, but no sound was coming out of his mouth. I continued, "You know, I've written letters to people that everyone said it was impossible to contact, and – may I add – even received replies. And then for an encore I managed to top it off. I worked so hard, pushed myself beyond my endurance, and had a stroke and ended up partly paralyzed for a while. But that was a few years back now." I found myself smiling at the absurdity of the story I was relaying, and yet it all was true. "My God, Robert, no one ever warned me that developing TRUITY would involve what I have been through."

Robert looked uncomfortable with what he was feeling. He ran his hand over his balding head as though reflecting upon what I had just said. Then, leaning back in his chair and taking a deep breath, he said, "Well, you always did have a knack for doing things in a way that was bigger than Ben-Hur," he laughed, ordering a cup of coffee from the waitress as she passed by the table. "But how did you do it? What happened? Where did the money come from?"

"You mean, how did I get from there to here? I suppose the answer is simple." I paused, thinking reflectively on the naive, enthusiastic person I used to be. "I never knew I couldn't." At that moment, I looked deeply into Robert's eyes, unafraid that he would see the truth of my statement.

"Bold as brass," my dad would have said. "More front than Myers."

"It just was not in my comprehension that I could not totally completely heal and reinvent my life while mapping the process so everyone else could use it." I found myself laughing almost uncontrollably. Must be the stress, I thought. "You know, when I left here, I think it probably was the fact that I was so naive and trusting. My belief in my life path was so strong a hundred wild horses couldn't have stopped me, truth be known."

I fiddled with the cup in my hand and placed it back on the saucer, looked once again straight towards my old friend sitting in the chair opposite me. "But I got to the finish line; I made it despite everything and everyone."

CHOICES BY T.B HUMAN™

Rob was shaking his head in disbelief, as though trying to take in the complexity of all that I had just said. "But, how did you learn to do what you have done? And what exactly is it anyway?"

"Do you know the biggest asset I had has been the fact I didn't know what I didn't know?" I leaned forward, tapping the table with my finger, "Because I didn't know how other people would have done it, I managed to achieve the impossible." Robert was smiling widely now, a gleam of light in his eyes as they showed he fully understood what I meant, without saying a word. "I simply held the vision in my mind of what I wanted to achieve, and just headed for it, one step at a time; I just started and kept going, no matter how hard it was, no matter how painful, I refused to give up or give in." I leaned forward, my right hand adjusting my watch, so I could see the time. "Have to be a story for another time, I'm afraid. I'm going to have to go." I pushed back the metal chair, straightening my black slacks and blue woolen coat as I did. The chair made an eerie scraping sound as I stepped aside.

"What about this weekend? Lunch on Saturday?" Rob asked. "I can't wait to hear what's happened. We'll have more time then, and no interruptions and distractions."

"Done," I replied, leaning forward and planting another kiss on his cheek as I stood moving forward to leave. "Oh, I'd better give you my address. You know Sandy Beach, don't you?"

Robert nodded. "Well, sort of," he replied.

"Well, just follow the main road in till you get to the beach, turn right and go to the end, and it's the second yellow villa in off the road."

"Easy, look forward to it," Robert replied.

Gathering up my shopping bags, I headed for the parking lot, smiling to myself as I walked through the crowd of people.

Saturday, 17th June 2002. Robert arrived about 12:25. It was a beautiful winter day. The sun shone, and a gentle breeze blew off the ocean, spreading a fine mist and the smell of sea air through the open house. In no time at all pleasantries over, and we settled down to a lunch fit for a king, chicken, salad and a platter of fresh sliced fruit. After eating our fill, we decided to retreat with our tea and coffee, to the upstairs lounge area where the sea views soothed the mind and the furniture sure did relax the body.

"Where did we finish the other day?" I asked.

"You were explaining to me how you managed to do so much," Robert replied. He stepped towards the green leather armchair and settled himself into its plush softness. "Hey," Robert began to laugh. "This lounge reclines. Wow." He fiddled with the arm cushions, continuing, "Absolute comfort. I can handle this." He was like a little boy, wriggling about in the chair, getting himself set for a long chat. That has always been one of Robert's precious qualities, enthusiasm for simple things. Life to him can be like the excitement of a little boy in a candy shop or a first kiss from his sweetheart. Meanwhile, I had settled back on the lounge, feet up and head propped up on one arm, totally relaxed and at peace with the world at large.

"Well, one thing I did find to be an integral part of what has happened was the fact I have always been fascinated by people who achieve success against the odds. You know, those who achieve in fields of creativity and humanitarian pursuits. People such as Nelson Mandela, Richard Branson, Michael Crawford, David Suzuki, Robert Redford, Bill Clinton, Sting, and Princess Diana, just to name a few, all of whom I believe to have shown immense courage, strength and belief in the fact that one person truly can make a difference in this world." I reached forward, taking a sip of the cup of tea I had brought with me from the lunch table. "Without having the pleasure of meeting these people they still became my guiding lights. I read everything I could on their lives and how they overcame the challenges life handed them. Their stories gave me strength and courage every time I felt I was about to go under." I sat back in the chair, looking absentmindedly out to sea. My mind pulled back the memories from ten years ago, still so vivid and clear, just as though they were yesterday.

CHOICES BY T.B HUMAN™

"I can remember saying to myself on many occasions, now, what would Branson do if he were in my shoes? You know, I must have written him twenty letters over a couple of years, and do you know what, he personally answered every one. I think for a man who is that busy that is really something, don't you?"

Robert nodded. "There aren't many out there who would bother, I bet."

Again, I began where I had left off. "After reading his book, *Losing My Virginity*, I concluded that Richard B and I had a lot in common, so I set out to try to meet him.

"After all, we came from the same space and almost the same place in the UK. His childhood was very much like mine in so many ways, and his challenges were similar in their structure, so I figured I had to be able to learn by his experience. If what he says in his book is correct, we both were lousy at school. I had dyslexia, and so did he, and we both sure do have creative minds; I just needed to work out how he started what he does, and copy it.

"So, I decided to take a leaf from his book, and I must admit I even adopted one of his pet phrases, 'Screw it, let's do it.'

"So, all in all, to sum up the last ten years I suppose you could say I have often enthusiastically rushed in where angels fear to tread." I roared with laughter, as scenes from the last years flooded into my mind. I recalled the huge bunch of daisies I had delivered to Michael C, and how Lynne, my friend and personal assistant, said he probably thought I was a stalker.

There was the bottle of Mentor red wine with the message wrapped around it we delivered back stage to John F, the TRUITY games sent to David Suzuki, Deepak Chopra, Robert Redford, Shirley McLain, and anyone else we could think of, including the Prince of Wales. As I spoke, I watched the bemused look on Robert's face turn to one of acceptance, and I continued. "God, we were either naive or very good at our marketing, not sure which, really." My gaze was taken back to the sea outside my window, as my mind tried to sort through the kaleidoscope of experiences from the last years. "When I think about it, Lynne and I did some totally nutty things. No one was safe from the marketing attempts of the TRUITY gang."

By now the tears had begun to roll down my face and I had to try to regain some composure, so I could fill Robert in on some of what I was laughing about. "But do you know what? to some extent everything I did worked."

"But how did you get to B?" Robert asked.

"Well, that's a story and a half. I sent him a message in a bottle."

"A what?" Robert looked puzzled, a wide grin spreading across his face. "There's got to be more to this one," he added, shaking his finger at me.

"You heard me; I wanted him to answer, so I figured if I sent him a 15-inch, bat-shaped bottle, with a glass painting of this silly little bean man running around the world on it, with a rolled paper message inside, it might just be nutty enough to get his attention, and it did. Oh, God, when I finally meet the man I sure will be embarrassed. Do you know we even sent him an Effie Doll once?" I was laughing so much that I could hardly contain myself.

"What's an Effie Doll?" asked Robert.

"It's a stress-management doll that I designed with a stupid poem on its chest. It's about 30cm high and bright yellow with long yellow plaits, and multicolored pants. She's real cute. But Richard didn't think so; it was the only letter I ever received back from him with 'Ms Halverson' as the intro." I shook my head. "I just wanted him to take the time to speak with me, and get some advice." By now I was talking so fast, I don't think poor Robert could get a word in edgewise.

"Each person I read about helped me to keep strong, and little by little I discovered the extra ingredients which I needed to develop, along with the skills and philosophy to build the person I am today." Robert nodded, still seeming to understand my train of thought. I continued the story. "I suppose when you think about it I had the courage to risk making an absolute ass of myself. I suppose it's that courage and my stretching the boundaries style of commitment to dare, combined with my passion to want to make a difference, that makes me. You know me; I have set my course to make the world a better place for my having been born, I suppose."

For a moment I stopped and reflected upon my words, thinking if I said them to anyone else but Robert, they would probably want to lock me up as a paranoid schizophrenic with delusions of grandeur. I laughed to myself at the thought, recalling the somewhat radical psychologist I had lived with for a short period of my life. "Let's not go there," I thought out loud to myself.

"The hard times certainly have been made somewhat bearable through the antics Lynne and I have put into action." It has always been exciting, never quite knowing who will answer our letters, and when."

By now Robert was in his thinking mode, hand under chin and tapping his cheek with his index finger. "But what was the point?" he shrugged. "What did you want to achieve?"

"Well, the brand TRUITY stands for freedom, and you know the board game I showed you downstairs, well, that's only one product using the concept that develops people's coping capacity, or stretches thinking in a positive and constructive way." Robert nodded as I spoke. I continued, "The word TRUITY actually means 'Truth Restores Understanding Increasing Trust – Yes.' Well, what I want to do is build a network where celebrities host TRUITY events to raise money for charity. You know, like Band-Aid from years ago, only bigger. I suppose to me it stands for the theory of we only have One World, and we're all a part of each other's existence."

"But how do you expect to do that?" Robert squirmed in his seat. "Boy! I wouldn't even know where to start something like that."

"Well, firstly you have to be bold; secondly, you can't take no for an answer; but most of all, you have to do it in a way that doesn't offend people, or become a nuisance. I suppose that's the guts of it."

"You know, years ago I always knew you would want to do something special. Robert picked up his cup of coffee and took a long slow drink; I don't even think he noticed it had gotten cold in the cup. He just sat there shaking his head and smiling.

"You know me, Rob; I have always wanted to do something that would make a real difference. Leave a legacy to mankind, that sort of thing. The total of the last twenty years has never been about the money, although I sure could do more to help people if I had some than I can with none." I shifted to become more comfortable in my seat. "That's why I developed TRUITY in the first place, so I could leverage my skills in personal development and emotional intelligence and give people something that could be a tool, a catalyst, for them to grow and change just as I have. And despite what some might think, it was never for the fame. All I have ever wanted to do is simply to make a difference and leave the world a better place for having been here."

CHOICES BY T.B HUMAN™

The day moved on, the sun was beginning to set behind the hills, and the cool evening air was beginning to descend and fill the room with its winter chill. We closed our day at that point. "Another cup of tea before you go?" I asked.

"Yeah, sure," Robert replied. You could see by the look on his face he was thinking deeply about all we had discussed. "You should write a book," he said.

"I have," I smiled back at him as we walked downstairs from the second floor of the villa. "In fact, I have written one fully, and have another three on the boil, and that's without all the training material and stress management and sensory development stuff I have written in the past," I added.

"Well, get them to the publisher. They're no good sitting on the shelf. I'm sure people would be fascinated that we have our own Louise Hay, right here in Oz."

I reached for the kettle and filled it with rain water from the second tap in the kitchen. "I have been going to do that, but I wanted to wait till I had TRUITY finished, and ready for the market, and my PR beginning to move."

"Well, what are you waiting for?" Robert was now leaning against the kitchen countertop, one arm holding him up precariously as he waved his index finger towards me, like a grandparent would do.

I laughed out loud. "Robert, there is no doubt you are food for the soul."

One and One Make Three

Thursday, 27th June 2002. Thank God, it's the 27th, the final transits of Saturn conjunct Pluto are over. Yea! Till one last blast early next year. Mercury is no longer retrograde in the heavens and we have just had our second lunar eclipse in two months, along with a partial solar eclipse. It is done! Once upon a time I believed that we could make things happen no matter may, for the sake of having you near." In hindsight, what a life I have had. No one would ever believe most of it, and love, yes, I have had love, but it never seems to stay. I always felt that there was a special someone out there that I had to find. How to have a husband without having a husband is what I call it.

I was married to Mac for twenty-three years and had several relationships which could have resulted in marriage, but my heart was my truth. And my heart screamed that the truth of the matter was no Mr. Right has crossed my path, not one who was single, anyway. The yearning deep inside me would just not go away. Someone from another time and place was calling me, and all I knew was it was tearing me apart to the point where I questioned my sanity.

I wasn't lonely, it was never that. It was more like I had had a husband and had left him in a bus station and couldn't remember which one.

However, right at this moment there is simply me myself and I sitting here in my home alone. Right at this moment I wonder at the complexity of it all, the

CHOICES BY T.B HUMAN™

last years. I question, "Have I missed my opportunity with whomever it is I search for because of my dedication to TRUITY?" My mum always said I was too fussy for my own good. Maybe it's me that has always had ideas above my station. I don't know. It seems as though I have spent most of my time searching for someone who has the capacity to be honest, have integrity, be a gentle soul and courageous and at the same time love as passionately and as truly as I do.

I am searching for a man that I can trust with my heart and soul, who would not reject me but protect and accept me for who and what I stand for. I never wanted someone to take care of me; I am far too fiercely independent for that. I just want someone who has their own life, yet is willing to stand behind me yelling from the sidelines, "Come on, girl. You can do it." I imagine him to have a sense of humor that borders on the ridiculous, and a depth of integrity, vision and passion that matches my own. I imagine that his love would take me to another world beyond the physical. I long for that world where time and space no longer exist. A world where I no longer search, a world where there is peace of heart. Yes, I am guilty of searching to find someone who would complement me and reflect my strength, someone above all, with the ability to love me without smothering me.

The CD clicks onto the next track, the song, "What a Girl Wants; What a Girl Needs." Music certainly has the ability to bring memories flooding back and at the same time provoke thinking of the future. He's got to be out there somewhere. I am fast approaching the big five-oh, and hell, I never thought it would take this long to find him. I suppose if you think about it, though, it's taken me this long to find out who I am, and what I stand for. I try to reassure myself that if I had met Mr. Synergy before, I probably would have stuffed it up; I sure am a different girl today than I was yesterday.

As Lynne would say, I have the ability to fall head over heels in love very quickly, my one weak spot. Being the friend, she is, she stands bewildered at some of my antics. I tend to see the good in everyone and trust far too easily and end up with my ego bent and wondering what the hell it was all about. That was, until one evening I met for the first time a certain gentleman. I walked into the room and my knees went weak, my heart raced, and my palms went to water. I looked across the room towards where he sat signing autographs and the world stopped. He looked up towards me and his mouth fell open and a shocked and stunned look spread across his face. Quickly he looked down to regain composure, but just as quickly he looked back, still unable to do anything but stare, mouth open. I fought back the tears and stood motionless unable to believe that this could happen.

It seemed like a lifetime passed in those twenty seconds, and Lynne stood chuckling beside me, saying, "You all right, dear?" She had that stupid smile of satisfaction on her face. "I told you, didn't I?" she gleamed. Minutes passed and finally we reached a space in the crowd where I could speak with him. Boldly, I held out my hand to shake his, and, taken aback, he was unable to speak. Something a bit like, "da,,da,,,mm," came out of his mouth as the people behind us pushed us forward. All too soon, the moment had passed.

CHOICES BY T.B HUMAN™

Bewildered and confused, I left the room, looking at Lynne and saying, "It can't be him! You must be joking. Now, how the hell is that ever going to happen?" And just to keep it interesting, life was still going to present me with, of all things, yes, another choice! Will you take this road, or that? It was like God spoke to me from the heavens saying, "Now you know your choices, you must first examine your life and then decide what your soul really wants, and – then and only then – you can have it."

So still wondering how this chapter will eventually come together, I just keep on keeping on. I certainly know he would match my passion and commitment, a rare and very special soul. I simply remind myself of the words of a wise old lady I know who would simply say. "What's meant for you, dear, won't go by you!" In this case, I sure hope she's right. A match made in heaven, I have no doubt. So now as our worlds coalesce, time will tell. Five years – a psychic in London once told me, I would have to wait five long years to find out. But that is another story, and Elton John sings out, "That's no sacrifice at all." It's timing; all of life is in the timing, and I had lots to do, and karma to complete before I would be ready.

The Processing Obsession

For years I have watched in awe at people who run from one workshop to another, searching for answers. Life is about balance, and so please keep in mind that it is not healthy to spend all your time trying to work out the reasons for your difficulties and problems. Simply put out the questions and allow nature to lead you to discover the insightful answers. Everything in life must be balanced in order that we have happy, healthy lives. A friend once said to me, "TRUITY, there are six aspects of your life you need to attend to every day. If you do you will be happy and healthy. You need to work, exercise, meditate, read inspirational literature, spend some time helping others and some time loving life and just having fun." Over the years I have truly come to understand the wisdom of his words.

Whenever we search for understanding, we push the insights we long for further away from us. I often found my need to understand something would drive me deeply into depression and seclusion. My balance would go out the window in the drive to find the answers and get to the end of the nightmare.

Eventually, I realized what was happening to me. With that awareness I became even more accepting of my process. One of the greatest realizations of all came to me when I understood how I disempowered myself with this process. I used the affirmation, "It is, simply because it is," to help me let go of my mind's need to understand everything. Ultimately, I understood that you don't need to understand why something is happening. When I began to practice openness to insight by using meditation and acceptance, my knowledge and ability to see the whole situation from a clear and truthful perception intensified. The thought processes involved in logical understanding simply project the memory of past events into the present and future by using words to paint a picture. When you reach the space where you trust yourself enough to be able to let go of trying to work it all out, you will see a whole different world around you.

CHOICES BY T.B HUMAN™

Our lives develop the most and our experience grows the fullness of our souls through our intimate relationships. The search for intimacy is something that eventually leads us all to experience the depths of ourselves within the reflection of another's presence, the drive of the "Wanabelong" people. The need to belong pushes us into places within ourselves that scare the hell out of us. But we must go there in order to find where we belong. Relationships show us the mirror of our own strengths and passions and reflect to us the projected perceptions which need to be healed, once and for all.

Back Where We Started, But in Another World: Caught in Groundhog Day

For those of you who have seen the movie *Groundhog Day*, I am sure you will have total empathy with this chapter of the story. For those who have not seen it, the storyline goes something like this: There was once this guy who moves to a small town where he is given the chance to live the same day over and over until he gets it right. Have you ever had one of those experiences that just keep happening in your life, and you find yourself thinking, Oh no! Not again! I thought I had learned this one. It's as though fate has given you the same lesson over and over and over again.

Right now, I am sitting here wondering what the hell this has all been about. I sense the wheel of life has turned full circle and that sooner or later all that we have gone through will make a lot of sense. The personal growth and the development of understanding in relation to human behavior has been enormous, but I sometimes wonder at the fact that humanity survives at all, considering that everyone seems to have a different agenda and almost everyone is out to do unto you before you do unto them. This is a sad fact, but true. Is it that I must rise to the challenge? Is it that being self-aware is not enough? If so, what is the challenge?

Back in the days of Number 62, I felt that simply being a good person with the desire to help and support the elimination of suffering was enough to get me through. I wrote a letter to Nelson Mandela. I wrote several, asking for an audience with the President.

CHOICES BY T.B HUMAN™

The strange thing about this time was that I knew there was a letter coming back from Nelson Mandela. I knew he had written or dictated a letter in reply to my request. Don't ask me how but I just knew there was a letter coming. Day after day I waited for the post to come and day after day I became more perplexed, thinking, wow, I got that one wrong. Six months later, the letter arrived, postmarked exactly six months earlier. The letter had taken exactly six months to travel from South Africa to Brisbane, Australia. What had happened? We will probably never know. Did some government department intercept the letter? Who knows? That letter getting lost cost me the opportunity to speak with the man personally. The opportunity was missed, and by the time the letter arrived here, Nelson was no longer the President of the Republic of South Africa and the connection was lost. Timing again, damn timing out again!

Once again, we face the missing mail syndrome. Unexplainably letters seem to vanish down a tunnel for a few weeks and then turn up. Well, some turn up; others, who knows?

CHOICES BY T.B HUMAN™

Walk a Mile in My Shoes

The wind blows, the waves crash constantly in the background, and it is cold and dark outside. Not a sign of life anywhere, but shortly the birds will begin their morning chorus and the dawn will break on another glorious day. I will once again walk the beach, drawing in its strength from the crystal blue waters and thundering surf.

The smell of that salt air – my, there is nothing like it on this earth. It fills me with peace; somehow it takes my soul to a place where everything just is. The time is 4:06 am, Tuesday, 24th July 2002, and once again I am woken from sleep, prompted to write another chapter in my new book. I woke thinking over the events of the last days, entwined with thoughts of the journey and the last few years. I could never have comprehended the knowledge, the growth and understanding this journey has brought into my life. I have found myself saying lately that if I had known what God had in store for me I probably never would have started all of this. I curled up in my warm cozy bed last night asking for guidance, help to see what I have not seen, help to understand the lack of tolerance in others and to find a way to restore peace and self-fulfillment in my life. I usually have peace; I sleep soundly always and have contentment with my lot, so to speak.

Lately, though, I seemed to have lost the plot, or taken a learning curve back into the realms of love. It's been a while since I explored this area of me, and it sure took me to the depths of my soul and left me wondering what on earth hit me. I know my mistake was to feel there was a safe place to rest. Loving someone brought back the reality of how hard it has been and reminded me of how long it has been since I could rest and feel I had come home. For so long, there has not been anyone beside me except trusty Wallace, bless her. Falling in love brought back the girl. Along with the girl, it brought the memories of vulnerability and the fear of hurt. It bought the idealistic and mostly far too trusting naiveté; it bought back all the subconscious doubts, all of which needed to be seen for what they were, relics of the past which had no foundation in my life today. The only way was to allow myself the discomfort of feeling, examining, and then letting go of the past.

Imagine for a moment that you journey with me: Imagine you have been traveling through the desert for twenty years, the sun has been searing you to the bone, everywhere you turn for shelter or safety turns out to be a place of pain and suffering, and you have nowhere to turn but inside yourself and to God. All your friends and loved ones who began the journey with you have passed away. They either gave up because the journey was too hard, or they have gone to do other things. The sun blasts down on you day after day, searing you to the bone; there is not one piece of you that has not been touched by the harshness and the inhospitality of the climate. Your legs and body are weary beyond comprehension; your mind longs for rest and safety. You know if you sleep, you are likely not to wake, for you are so tired and exhausted. Finally, you find your oasis, the place of your dreams, a safe haven set amongst an unfriendly world, and you just long to rest and have someone else watch over you so you can recharge and continue the journey to its end.

CHOICES BY T.B HUMAN™

At the age of 27, I began this epitaph, searching for understanding and for acceptance in this world and of this world. I began the journey into my desert or what some call the book of shadows. I would face the deepest, darkest corners of my own soul and from that learn about me and the true nature of my soul, and the courage and strength I have that few others seem to possess. As a child, I was an extreme sensitive. Living in the bush seemed to develop within me a sense of intuition that in my later years has become quite profound. During my years as a young woman, the intuition was clouded by the insecurities of being thrust into marriage and motherhood at the age of sixteen. Yet many years later, after losing my confidence and trust in myself and giving that to someone who really didn't deserve it, and who certainly did not walk a spiritual path, in the life as an older, wiser mother and grandmother, the same belief that I was born to do something special drives me into realms and striving to achieve in a way few will ever truly understand. I am a complex and yet simple person. I have such extremes of sensitivity to other people's situations that I can always walk a mile in another person's shoes.

I have empathy and the ability to see the root cause of problems swiftly and clearly, and from that I have always been able to stretch those boundaries in a way to help others find solutions. The hard part of this, when I was younger, was that I felt and saw the heartache of society so deeply that I wanted to do something about it all, to make a difference.

That was and still is who I am. Older now, for sure, and wiser, although sometimes I wonder. The journey into developing the brand of TRUITY has not passed without cost, personal, financial and physical. The cost has brought with it change so massive that at times I feel totally overwhelmed that people still and never will really see the extent of how I have grown and changed. They forget I could hardly read and write. People forget I have no formal education, they forget the immensity of the challenge to keep on despite every challenge presented. Life would appear to create situations where people get so caught up in survival they forget the essence of life is what is of real importance. They leave the search for truth and for the development of concepts which will help the world to everyone else, and after my journey I can understand why they make this choice. When my journey turns the corner, I have no doubt at that point suddenly I will be surrounded by support from long-lost friends. I have no doubt some of those people will be people that I never knew existed. And that is life.

I have learned that people have somewhat unrealistic expectations of you once you have achieved something like TRUITY. For some strange reason they no longer allow you the luxury of being human. Somehow, you become superhuman, and then if you dare to show you are just the same as they are, and get upset or angry, they retaliate with acid like venom which would burn through the heart of the bravest of heroes. I remember the Dalai Lama saying exactly the same thing, "People do not allow me the luxury of being human, and having normal human emotions. And after all, I am just a man, an ordinary man who has the same feelings and fears as everyone else."

CHOICES BY T.B HUMAN™

I have learned that when ones shows vulnerability it seems to frighten others. I am not sure if it's the result of seeing their own reflection in your actions or exactly what it is. I only know that the very minute I show others I am human, immediately I'm judged and cast out as being a fake and daring to show I am anything less than perfect. I recall days in the office where the mental and emotional stresses upon me were enormous; my stress levels were higher than Mount Everest. I was literally screaming inside for help; my moods were volatile, my endurance stretched to the limit. But did I get understanding and help from my staff? Even when I sat them down and said, "I am not coping. My upset is about me, not you," they did not understand. My staff sent back words and actions to whip me like, "You invented TRUITY; you should practice what you preach." I expected more, couldn't they see I was shattering into a million pieces? Their lack of understanding and compassion whipped me more and more.

I understand they accept their own distress at the time of change and chaos. Why is it that people don't know how to accept each other in times of need? Why is it they cannot accept that I, too, am growing and look for safe harbor through the storms?

My thoughts this evening were triggered by a friend commenting to me that I should go back and read my first book, that "The girl who wrote it was really switched on," he said. Now, does this mean I am not switched on now? I am not sure, hence the self-questioning and the early morning clarity emerging like a butterfly from its cocoon. I wonder often at people's willingness to judge, their willingness to jump to conclusions as to what you should be doing or what is wrong with your life without even for one moment extending the hand of compassion, tolerance and unconditional love. I wonder if anyone else could have endured the pressure and challenges I have faced in the journey I have taken. I wonder if they would still have the passion and love for humanity, if they had been treated as I have. I wonder if they would still turn to God in the wee small hours of the morning when it seemed that God was nowhere to be found?

Walk a mile in my shoes is like Nelson Mandela's, story, *Long Walk to Freedom*. His story gives precious glimpses, and glimpses only, of his journey. He shares with us the events and insights gathered along the way, and yet when reading it I felt that there was so much more, so much that could not be encapsulated by the words of the story. What is in my heart is far more than any book can ever tell, for what is in my heart is an incredible love and dedication to humanity, even though right at this moment I don't like people very much.

You may think that a contradiction. Yes, it is. I don't like the way people expect you to be something no one can be; I don't like the fact they treat each other with such a lack of respect and understanding. I don't like it that they are such selfish creatures. To find out if a friend is true, tell them that you cannot give them what they want and see how many friends you have left. I used to think I had a lot of friends. Now I understand I have a lot of acquaintances. My friends only wanted me for a friend when I had something to give them, be it time, advice, support, love, a place to stay, whatever.

When I became busy with TRUITY, my friends could not lean on me as much. I was not there to tell them how to help themselves and spend hours helping them turn their lives around. They could not see what I was trying to achieve for everyone. They walked away because they did not feel special anymore. They could not have what they wanted, because at the end of the day there was simply nothing left of me to have. They did not understand that the sacrifice I brought into my life was for them, and it was my choice to help the many, not the one.

Another Clue

The giant puzzle of what on earth life was about was beginning to unfold; already my life was changing day by day. I had dared to question! I had questioned my very existence within the scheme of things; there was no going back now. I was born an intuitive, but now I began to embrace the fact that I had to learn how to harness that power, that knowing, and no longer be afraid of it or what people thought about it. I knew the more I developed my sixth sense or, intuitive abilities, the more complex and yet simple life had to become for me. My nature is to be open about life. I am not one for manipulative games or secrets, and with me what you see is what you get.

I never thought that for one moment my openness would end up subjecting me to such a horrendous twenty-year barrage of negative energy. What I didn't understand is that when you allow other people to know, they have the opportunity to contaminate your life with their thoughts and opinions. If I had kept my own counsel I have no doubt the road would have been much smoother and the journey not nearly as devastating or challenging. However, in true TRUITY form, it seems I wanted to survive the maximum challenge. So, without even realizing it, I put up the flag and said, "Come get me. You won't hurt me!" People often judged my openness to life as being irresponsible or naive. My extreme vulnerability seemed to challenge people to the point they just wanted to kill me off. To this day, however, I still believe my openness was and is my greatest strength. I thought people would just understand me and accept me and encourage me to keep on with my life and my desire to help others.

The only problem was, I never felt like I belonged anywhere, and I must admit the need to belong and be a part of the group would very nearly be my undoing. I turned more and more to my inner sense of guidance. My dreams informed me, and my waking moments brought insight into events and understanding of the path I had chosen to walk. I came to know myself better than anyone else, and with that sense of knowing, slowly I developed a trust in my choices.

What was once so complex had become so simple. Somehow, I was returning to innocence. I seemed to be developing a sense of play and happiness inside of me that adults just couldn't fathom. I only realized this from spending time sitting watching my grandchildren play. I had to laugh when I realized I had just spent the last ten years desperately trying to learn to do what my young grandchildren naturally do. As I watched, my grandchildren fought and struggled with each other, got completely lost in the drama, and then in an instant were giggling and playing as though nothing had happened. I was learning to be in the now, to let go of the memories, the garbage, the rigid beliefs and just live life – now!

As I watched, it became obvious their problems rarely lasted for more than a moment or two. They would move swiftly from one situation to another, never staying long in any space. Children have a wonderful ability to ask direct and often obvious questions. Sometimes we as adults could die of embarrassment at their openness and honesty, but in doing so they nearly always get the information they need. Children are unconditionally trusting of someone they love. Even if that person hurts them, they forgive and forget quickly. It is only with age we seem to forget how to accept change. Children do not have beliefs to get in the way of their achieving. A child will imagine they can fly a plane, slay a dragon and conquer the universe, all in one afternoon. And they probably would do those things, if we supported their belief in themselves.

When a child is young it does not take life seriously. As long as a child's immediate needs are taken care of, they don't have a worry in the world. Children start their lives being in the world but not of the world. As they grow, they learn to be of the world, until, ultimately, they must once again get back to where they started, in the world but not of the world.

We spend far too much time telling our children what they are doing wrong, rather than pointing out their strengths and good points. Our children can achieve anything in the world if they have a good sense of self worth. Every time we tell them they are stupid, they are bad, or they are dumb, we damage their ability to risk taking a chance. Each child has a unique skill and talent. Some are good at sports, while others are good students. Please remember they cannot all be good at all things. Find out their special talent, and then encourage and support them every step of the way to achieve in that arena. no matter what it is. Not everyone can be bank managers or brain surgeons. There is room for all sorts of people in this world, and it would be a far happier place if we could somehow do the impossible and have our future generations working at what they loved instead of doing jobs they hate.

CHOICES BY T.B HUMAN™

23rd November 2002. Today things are tough, more difficult than ever before. I must find a way to keep the vision alive, and I must believe this has all been for a purpose. It certainly has strengthened me, and opened my eyes. My daughter was walking with me on the beach just yesterday, and her comments were, "Mum, do you know why this has all happened?" I answered that I wished I did. "Well," she said, "you have always been too understanding, too gentle and accepting, you always see everyone's point of view and end up feeling you have to be the one who is wrong, and that's not true. You had to experience this because if TRUITY had flown before, you would have given it all away. You had to see people for what they truly are in order to use what God is about to give you wisely, and I know it has been hard, but it had to happen. You simply trust too much, and you trust people with you far too much. Mum, you are worth the best, and out there somewhere is a man who is equal to you and will be proud to walk by your side." The tears ran down my face as I wondered at the wisdom of my daughter, so precious, so wise and just like her mother, finds it so difficult to find a safe place in this world to rest. So, for now we rest with each other. Acceptance we have, trust we have, far stronger than anyone could imagine, and love, well, there's tons of that to go around. I have been blessed and somewhere and somehow God has granted me the blessing of three wonderfully wise children.

When things are tough, and money is scarce, sadly once again I find that my friends are in even shorter supply than any other time in my life. Everyone is gone. Only the memories remain, and life is pretty empty right about now. I have a sense it's going to get worse before it gets better. I suppose the way to explain it is that people seem to feed off each other, not a pretty sight but often sadly true. They want you for what they can get out of you. They only want to know you when life is good. I have always filled my life with helping others. I have honestly questioned at times whether I have done this to feel I have some value to this world. Has it been my need to be needed that has driven me? I understand how my true spiritual wisdom has brought with it an immense cost. My life has been stripped bare of everything that is not real; all that remains is the essence of me, my love for my family and some select friends, and the passion and purpose which TRUITY brings to me and the Choices it brings to people. There is, at times, an overwhelming sense of isolation, and yet the peace within me grows stronger as I know myself on other levels. In hindsight, I can see that my journey to blend the unconscious with the conscious, in a tangible and practical form, has brought me peace. The journey has brought with it the lessons of compassion, tolerance, love, and, above all, the ability to question my motivation with the utmost honesty. The more spiritually in tune one becomes, the more the child-like qualities of trust and naiveté emerge. The world would have us believe, however, that these qualities indicate we are naive and incompetent. Well, haven't they got a surprise coming? In the words of His Holiness the Dalai Lama, "Even I get angry sometimes, and people think I am terrible for it. They forget, above all, that I am human."

Start Spreading the News

It is difficult to explain the events of the past weeks; time and time again we have had the finish line within our grasp only to have it whisked away in a hurricane of disbelief and confusion. It would seem the universe is against us, for some odd obscure reason. It would appear to all be a matter of timing. However, despite having no money or support, we, or rather I, somehow find the strength just to keep going. Poor Lynne and David just stand by and give whatever moral support they can, and at times I have no doubt that the hell they have experienced is in close proximity to my own experience.

When faced with situations where the heart, the mind and the soul are so confronted with one brick wall after another one has no choice but to turn inwards and seek out the deepest, darkest truth of the soul. Funny thing is, when I checked my astrological charts for the past couple of years, and the transits I have just moved through, it is no wonder that the challenge has been so profound. Saturn opposition Pluto with mercury retrograde – life and death stuff.

The best way I can explain is, if you think of Saturn as the teacher with the big stick, and Pluto as power in the physical world and karma, then add to that Mercury as communication and moving forward with projects, well, that about says it all. The universe would not allow me to move forward until I had turned my focus inside to check that what I do is for the right reason, and that the power and the success which come from that will be used appropriately. I was born with chart aspects which indicate I am destined to become a high-profile public person who is a world leader in the field of humanitarian pursuits. I have always been a firm believer in the theory that what we began we must finish, and that life after life we move forward in the pursuit of doing just that, pulling to us the elements and challenges in order to complete what we originally set forth to do.

The Lunar Eclipse 25th June 2002

Yesterday was another day fraught with disappointments and inner challenges. The day began with the news arriving that the television appearances had once again been put back. This is the second time this has happened now. The tragedy is that we are running so close to losing everything that I have worked so hard to achieve. We have needed that big break, or should I say the opportunity for the door to open and for me to get some public exposure. I feel like a rubber band that has been strung out so tightly that God only knows what will happen when it is set loose. In the meantime, however, I just pray that somehow it is made of strong enough material that it does not snap.

My first reaction to the news was absolute devastation; I could have in that moment sought to end my life. If I were not such a strong person, with such strong belief in my life path, I probably would have. I can understand how the branch of life can simply break under the pressure of such bewildering and soul-shattering obstacles. However, the sense of purpose stayed strong within me, and it was not long before I had bounced back and put the whole situation into perspective. I responded to the PR man with, "Well, what do we do in the meantime? What now? I don't have the luxury of time on my side. The ball is in your court."

Earlier that day I had been speaking with a friend who is a media person in the neighborhood, and in our conversation, I turned to him for advice. "David, who is there locally who I can contact to get some advice or support? You have gotten to know me by now, and I suppose I see you as knowing the personalities in the district and knowing me and what I am about. I have this terrible feeling that the media thing is going to be cancelled and I am running so close to the wind that I need some help. I have never been good at asking for help, but I must find a way through this. I need a mentor. Someone to take me under his or her wing and open the doors for me. Is there someone you could introduce me to? I need some publicity and fast." David's response was to suggest that I contact George and his wife Kirsten. I related the story of how George had been the very first person I had written to many years before, when I started TRUITY. No matter how polite the letters, he never responded to my approach. Anyway, David suggested we have a try now. He could show them the tape that we had been working on. After all, we had nothing to lose. They could only say yes or no. The day moved on with dentist appointments and just the normal day-to-day things of cooking and cleaning and trying not to drive myself crazy with the worry of the situation.

CHOICES BY T.B HUMAN™

While I kept reminding myself that someone upstairs (God), must know what they are doing, my gut feeling kept saying that something unforeseen was about to unfold which would bring a positive resolution to the situation.

It's a strange feeling to know things are going to work out all right when you're in the midst of utter chaos, with people banging on the door wanting to be paid, and not knowing where the next week's rent is coming from, let alone the answer to the situation at hand. Evening came, and with it brought the strength of spirit once again to be positive and move forwards another step.

How did I get from there to here? I suppose the answer is simple. I never knew I couldn't. "Where is 'here'?" you may ask. Well, my world is about to change forever; all that I worked towards and struggled to achieve is now once again nearing the ends of my fingertips.

All a Matter of Attitude

Attitude. Well, my attitude has always been one of keeping on no matter what, and to turn every obstacle into an opportunity. Sometimes, I have kept going grudgingly, I must admit, but for the most part I have just been head down and bottom up. Each step has meant an extension of my skills and practical abilities to achieve. So many people give up their dream just when success is about to happen. It just gets too hard. When is it madness and when is it right to keep working towards your goal? When is enough, enough?

In the days which were to follow I had to make some of the hardest decisions of my life. I had to face the fact that I had been wrong in following the branding name change; I had to face the fact that because of my naiveté, my financial arrangement with David had been under his control. He had doled the money out in tiny bits, never allowing me the financial strength to achieve my goals. Now I was faced with a warehouse full of product and no way of marketing it, because it was incorrectly labeled. I had learned so much, but only in hindsight. To top it off, the business partner who was going to come on board to market and get the product off the ground had a change of life circumstances when his wife developed cancer. Our business partnership was never realized, and I was left high and dry. I was not willing to take the risk of running up debts without knowing that I could pay them, so the office was closed, and things were put on hold. In the end, after battling for a year and a half to get some help here in Australia I had no choice but to find someone who was willing to assume the financial losses of the company and provide the financial assistance to appoint a liquidator and clear up this whole damn mess. Even though it was a relatively small mess of $30,000 it was still beyond what I could raise, and no one would help me. The banks would not help, friends would not help, and there was no one at that point in time. I thought it was the worst day of my life the day I signed those papers. I felt as though my heart was breaking into a thousand pieces and that it was the end of me and the twenty years of work I had put into TRUITY.

I know I could have not learned any other way but to have been in it. As my mum would have said it's better to learn your lesson with pennies rather than pounds, and the future potential of the product range was certainly enormous compared to what we had first envisioned. That is something only the reader can ultimately decide. There have been many times I have literally screamed, "I can't take any more; it's too hard." But somehow the heroine inside me helps me find the strength to keep on. Why am I so driven? For me the answer was that I truly believe in my vision, and my vision was never about the money; it was always about people. All I ever wanted to do was give people a choice, to give them the tools to develop their capacity to be supportive and constructive. My vision and the TRUITY brand symbolize choices, "A hand up and not a handout." A brand which represents freedom.

So, I stand in the fire of my challenge and realize the challenges have been blessings in disguise. Today, I don't blink an eye when it comes to preparing documents, business plans and speaking with people of power. The events of the last years have been God's preparation ground, things sent to test my mettle, so to speak. Today I listen to with my mind, body and heart to what is happening around me. I no longer take no as a personal rejection. It simply makes me ask, well, where did I fall down; what more do I need to master? The business of TRUITY had challenged me thick and fast, and if I had believed what well-meaning souls advised me back in the beginning, none of what you are about to read would have even been experienced. I would have simply gone out and got a job.

From the ashes, after the fire sale, came new light. The company was resolved in a matter of weeks, there was very little to pay out, and all in all people were understanding and compassionate. I pulled myself together, and with the help of God, kept on keeping on, only by the skin of my teeth, I must admit, but it's okay, and that's what's important.

I knuckled down and finished the workbooks and products designs. I rose to the challenge and developed the business plan and financial forecasts, and now I am out there again, looking for an investor to see this vision though, and it will happen, of that I have no doubt.

CHOICES BY T.B HUMAN™

All the emotions, all the insecurities have now left me. Nothing has changed, but everything has changed. Ultimately, I believe that what I must give this world this world needs, and with that I have the courage to go all the way. I had to learn to do it by the book, prepare documents, do the numbers and present my ideas so anyone could pick them up and see my vision. That was a part of my challenge. In recent weeks I have gone out there on a limb one more time. I placed an advertisement for venture capital on a board in the United States, and guess what? Not one, not two, but seven offers came in as a result. Seven of the world's top venture capital firms have offered me the millions I need to go the next step. I have come from a girl that no one would take seriously to this, simply because I was willing to face the challenge head on, and not give up no matter what. The papers are on my computer waiting for signature now as I type this last entry into the book.

The lunacy of the situation was that last week my lease on my home was terminated by a bad-natured real estate agent because I was two weeks late with my rent. It didn't matter to them that I paid in advance for years, so, Beth, I hope your face is red with the embarrassment of knowing the extra pressure they placed upon me that day.

At the same time, others who I am indebted to have let me struggle and keep going without pressing unduly for payment, and for that I give thanks. It has been a year from hell, but would I have missed it? No, not for anything. I have risen to the challenge, and in doing so know what I am capable of doing and achieving, and that I don't have to take life personally.

I live life to the best, I tell my children I love them, I hug my grandchildren and help build their dreams and confidence in who they are capable of becoming, and if I am wrong I have the courage and strength to say I'm sorry. I don't take today's problems into tomorrow; life is too short and people too precious. I address the issues when they happen, and with constructive approach, and above all I trust in God to show me the way. I listen to the beating of the heart of this world and have the courage to keep going.

CHOICES BY T.B HUMAN™

3rd March 2003. My God, it's so simple. All the years I have wondered what the secret is that I knew I held inside of me, all those years of trying to work out what the meaning of life is. Life is simple. The choices we make take us to the experiences we need to heal, and in the healing often the pain and suffering comes from the infection being lanced to let the poison out, just like a wound that has been festering deep within the skin. I have been led constantly by my trust in God. Some may be more comfortable with calling this my quest to heal my life, my personal development, or my "Choices." Whatever you want to call the motivation is irrelevant; the fact is, a deep calling within my psyche has influenced me. The result of this is that I have had to stand in the fire of my passion, and the result has been self-purification. I know myself, my weaknesses, my strengths, and from that point I can make clear choices as to my next steps into the unknown. Through this passage I have learned a few essential techniques which support my continued growth and the continual acceptance and deprogramming of my fears.

My subconscious and conscious choices led me to feel the frustration, the anger, the pain and eventually to know myself better than anyone else in this world. It is this knowing which finally released the beliefs that were inappropriate to my life. So many times, I found myself going to the depths of my soul, wondering if this would ever stop, and yet, each time I would reemerge with clarity so profound that it was awesome. Life really is like the Billy Connelly movie, *The Man Who Sued God*. It is as though some magic hand takes us to where we don't want to go in order for us to find what we most need inside of us. In doing so, we let go of all the beliefs which are inappropriate. The beliefs that I had taken on had to do with poverty, and so I kept manifesting poverty and the struggle until I realized it was all an illusion.

Today that illusion has shattered. I sit here, one hand empty, no money to speak of, and the other hand holding millions. My accountant tells me that when the venture capital deal is finalized, I will instantly become, on paper anyway, a multimillionaire. Holding exact opposites within the same space, once again I knew I had released the karma, the mind patterns, the beliefs that had kept me recreating poverty. It's done! Along with a dozen other patterns of life that I now realize will never come again.

A Letter to a Friend, 7th March 2003

I wrote:
My dearest friend, you are in my thoughts tonight as I sit and write. My heart goes out to you and I wish I could just tuck you up in a big, warm blanket and make you a hot chocolate and let you cry away your tears. The court case with your ex-husband was not what it seemed. The fact that you were the one to catch him out, and that you were the one who brought the attention to him of having committed the assault on your granddaughter has provoked you to take a journey to the depths of your soul. God provided a vehicle where you would go and feel the pain where you didn't want to go. The pain of your own childhood, the anger, the overwhelming helplessness, the lack of justice, which you felt as a child, has all been brought to the surface. I know it's hard to understand, and right at this moment you feel that God has betrayed you, but, my friend, he has given you the greatest gift of all.

CHOICES BY T.B HUMAN™

He has taken you to the depths in order that you feel all that you have been denying, and from here your life will heal.

There is a method I used with my clients in therapy many years ago, and I still use it with myself today and that is allowing myself to just feel what I am feeling without putting words to it. Feel the anger, the pain, the injustice all the emotions of the child within you who screams for justice. Embrace the pain, draw it into your body and look it in the eye, and know there is nothing to fear anymore. You have stood up, in front of God, your family, and the law and had the courage to speak out about things that happened. You did this with clarity and you mastered your emotions and spoke with the detachment of a healed person. Your inner child has spoken the unspeakable; you have done so much more than you will ever know by speaking out with clarity and holding your truth as your protection. I am proud of you.

Try not to become angry and bitter. It's time to let it all go so that you can now bring a man into your life who will honor you for the wonderful woman you are. The karma is released, and your family will never have to walk this path again. It has not all been about justice; it has also been about healing and reclaiming your power as a woman, and this you have done. Acknowledge the healing. You have reclaimed a piece of you, and in doing so a false part of you has died, and that is the grief you have felt the last days. I have had this happen many times. It's as though I journeyed into my emotions, but I didn't. Nor will you. You are strong, you are brave, and you want to live and love life to the fullest. Trust yourself, and trust my words, it is only an old damaged part of you that is dying and leaving because you don't need that part anymore. It's like an astral body leaving; there is always a feeling of shock and trauma when this happens.

Think about what I have written, for it is the truth, and you know I always speak the truth, my friend. I love you dearly and do so wish I could be there for you to wrap you up and let you rest and rebalance after your incredible journey.

I am so proud of you, and that you are my friend. Don't worry about your ex-husband. God has a way of evening things out, and I have no doubt the repercussions upon his life will be like ripples of a stone being thrown upon the water. His family may have appeared to side with him in court, but do you think behind closed doors they will let him persist with his behavior? I think not.

Trust in God to take care of this now. Take care of yourself. All I ask is that you think about what I have written. God bless.

The Alien Connection

Have you ever stopped and thought seriously about the theory of an alien connection to this planet? To my way of thinking, there is a multitude of ways codependence manifests itself, and the determination of individuals to avoid taking a good honest look at themselves can be disguised by thinking or wanting someone else to blame or be responsible for our rescue. The human mind has an unlimited capacity to create and project incredibly complex scenarios, all in the name of justifying our existence, our actions and our belief structures.

We often are so involved with the drama that it is not often that we are given the chance to step back and take a good look at the bigger picture. When you do step back sometimes it's shocking what you discover about yourself and those around you. People generally are well intentioned, and not many people are evil or deliberately nasty. The alien conspiracy I would describe in two ways. It seems to be on one hand all these people who are waiting for someone to rescue them from the mess we have made of this world. Or on the other hand there are those who fear the presence of anything alien, convinced they are the primary source of evil and are to be feared. Alien: What does the word conjure up for you? To me alien implies something foreign or not fully understood, something beyond comprehension. Well, I feel this world is full of aliens. No, I don't mean the ET type. What I am talking about here is humanity.

Do you think the way humans treat each other is normal? Do you consider life on this planet to be normal? I understand the more I watch the way humanity is evolving the more bewildering it becomes. For it seems to injure, steal, murder, and in general not to be responsible for your life is extremely alien. So, who are the aliens, they or we? And if you were an alien from a superior race would you want to mess up your planet by helping us?

Getting back to the first scenario, or the rescue syndrome: It appears rescue or the desire to have someone or something come and save us from ourselves is one of the more prominent New Age, old age, perceptions of alien life's purpose. I have no doubt at all there are other forms of life besides human beings. But to me, the whole well publicized concept of some giant galactic rescue has never made any real sense. After all, if you were another intelligent, evolved race of beings, who were happy, healthy and aware, would you want to come to earth and take humans back with you to mess up and pollute your world just like we have messed up ours? I don't think that it is very likely, do you? I do believe that in all probability there are other races of beings that are knowingly assisting the consciousness of human beings to grow. I do believe it is possible they have sensed and responded to our cries for assistance, but like all good teachers they simply supply the clues and we must work it out for ourselves.

They will not give us the answers or solve our problems; if they did we would never learn the lesson. I don't believe there is, or ever will be, any rescue party arriving. No one is going to do it for us. I am afraid the responsibility stops with us. I am well aware of how convenient some beliefs can be. I am also aware of how convincing illusions can be, especially when you are in the midst of them. After all, I have briefly embraced most of them at some time or other, on my journey from there to here, just like the rest of you. As a race of people, we created this experience that we call life, to have the chance to ultimately get *It* clear, to learn how to blossom and live in tune within ourselves so this environment and our lives will flourish.

The second scenario is the one where the aliens are the "baddies." I would suggest anyone who thinks like this simply look outside at what we are doing to ourselves, and then have a second thought about the whole situation. Human beings have the capacity to achieve so much and yet so much of the energy here on earth is used for self-gain and self-importance.

We are all interconnected, a part of one being, one universe. Remember what I said about the universe – one song. As my friend once said to me, it seems to be a natural thing that the blood flow is less in some areas of the body than in other parts. In a world where there is so much, why is it that, so many have so little? Why is it we no longer feel safe to smile and say hello to a stranger? Who, I ask you, are the aliens?

Somewhere Along the Path

It is now the middle of winter, and a great deal of time has passed since I began this manuscript and my awakening. For a moment my attention is taken by my surroundings, and I glance around my bedroom-cum-office. My goodness, a lot has happened in the last years. I moved home to the central coast of New South Wales to be with my family two years ago now.

CHOICES BY T.B HUMAN™

During the years at Number 62, I missed walking in the sunshine and looking at the sea, playing with my grandchildren and seeing my children grow into wonderful people. However, in the time since I have come back I have healed so much and let go of so much that words cannot describe. Yes, it has been a difficult time. It has been a year of losing everything I owned, being let down in ways that could not have been comprehended, being driven to stand my ground in ways I never knew existed. It's been a full-on time of grieving, grieving all that has been and the choices I made for the wrong reasons.

Now the time of grieving has passed, and it is once again time to move on with my life, to let go and let God lead me to new directions, to utilize my experience in ways that I probably could never have comprehended. Spring is coming and with it the life I have struggled and prepared for. The time has come and with it will be love and fulfillment. The mists have cleared, and life is about to begin anew. What a wonderful experience it has all been. I am not a religious person. I would say I am a person who has a keen mind and thorough openness and honesty. I have developed a balanced, healthy respect for all belief structures and philosophies. I don't know if there is an adequate word to describe me. I always feel words limit our reality. This belief is colored by the fact that we all have individual perceptions and beliefs attached to each of the words we use. However, as I sought deeper understanding of how I could develop such a tool, I kept remembering the words from the Bible, "Be ye all as little children who come unto me," and I found myself thinking about those words more and more. Somehow, I sense I have managed to return to innocence, in that I have learned to live life once again. This time I don't drag the past behind me; things are worked through fast and smooth, and life moves on.

Karma, Karma, Who's Got the Karma?

I am aware of the need every individual must walk their own path, but, gee, it would have been easier if there was someone out there holding a light or an axe to chop down some of the trees in my way. Living brings on the challenges; it's in the doing we learn from the experiences we create through the choices we make. Our karma or lessons in life are intertwined with our subconscious beliefs and our genetic blueprint. I don't really believe in karma. Unless you are ignoring your knowing, how can it be that you have karma? You have choices, and whether those choices are made in this life or in another time, it's all just experience. All the influences intertwine with our social structure or culture, our values, our beliefs, our goals and life experience. The result, however, is whatever we experience, be it joy or suffering. Everything is a direct result of the choices we consciously or unconsciously make, and it's that simple. Life wakes us up, one way or another. It pushes, it entices, it overwhelms us, all so that we will gain more awareness about how our choices and actions create our experience. Once again, the challenge is and always will be to be self-honest during the experience. If you can do this, then your journey is fast and your growth profound, or at least that's how I have experienced life.

Have you ever said yes to someone when you wanted to say no? I bet you have. Whenever you do this, karma comes into play. Why did you say yes when you wanted to say no? That is the question. Was it because you didn't want to hurt the other person or was it because you were afraid of what might happen if you said no? Early in my life I began asking myself some honest questions and the result is that I have had to have the courage to find a way to live that honesty; in everything I do, one hundred percent of the time.

I was once told that karma, meaning the belief that we have a debt to repay is not true. If you speak of karma as what goes around comes around, then that I have found is true. If you believe you have a debt to repay, you will attempt to repay it. If you believe you are unworthy of love, you will create rejection. If you believe you are bad, you will attempt to prove to everyone you are the nicest person in the world. Our karma, or lessons, cease the moment we become aware, the moment we realize we are doing something or believing something that supports the creation of the difficulty. The moment we become aware we are doing whatever it is, our future options change, and we have learned from the experience.

CHOICES BY T.B HUMAN™

There are indeed many roads to enlightenment, and eventually everyone will consciously arrive. Whether it be by accident or by design, we will all become enlightened eventually.

We are so desperate to learn. Because most of our lives are not comfortable, we often mistakenly take on another person's beliefs thinking they have some secret knowledge. This illusion creates learning, along with a great deal of unnecessary confusion along the path. It can also make the manipulator a great deal of money.

One of the greatest fears that accompanies change, one we all must face, is the fear that we will lose those we love. Love is the only thing you can take with you when you leave this world. Love cannot be damaged, broken or destroyed. Love is the eternal essence of you. The only things that can cloud it or overshadow it are the beliefs we hold to as individuals.

CHOICES BY T.B HUMAN™

The Greatest Illusion of All

The pain and fear we feel when our physical security is threatened is something we all have experienced at some time or other. When I faced that demon, I clung to the thought that I would get through this time. I wanted to believe that my security came from within me, but I was so scared. I felt way out of my depth and I had no one to give me the solid financial advice of how to get to the end of the nightmare. I began isolating myself from the world, in order to feel safe, but somehow, the world kept breaking through. My self-protection was chaining me to the experience, and I just kept on experiencing Groundhog Day.

Things were not moving ahead in a way that supported positive outcomes. I placed far too much emphasis on getting rid of the things I had accumulated, like ornaments, memorabilia, books, utensils and even furniture. I felt the overwhelming need to lighten the load, in every way possible. Anything I had been given by anyone about whom I had a bad memory was given away or sold at garage sales. I read somewhere about the effects of subconscious memory upon our ability to heal our lives, so everything went. I had little or no money in the bank and I prayed a lot. I knew that my security would come not from money in the bank but from my ability to create money on a daily basis.

The problem was that I had spent so much time working out how to leverage my knowledge and developing the product range, that I had lost touch with the reality of daily survival and my daily financial income requirements. The ship was sinking, and I was still not going to admit that I was in trouble.

I knew I had the ability to get through; I just didn't have a clue how! The only thing I could do was to go back to the principles of basic personal development. I just kept on moving forward, doing one thing every day to get closer to my end goals. I meditated, I rested, I fought the fight of the effects of the extreme stress I was placing upon my body, mind and soul, and I prayed.

CHOICES BY T.B HUMAN™

I looked at my values and my beliefs, and to be totally honest and open, I often spent hours crying at the sadness that had become my life. I felt abandoned and cut off, a victim of my own making, and yet I could not abandon the project. I knew it was meant to be, and that it had the power to change people's lives for the better. It was just a pity that here I was the creator of the method and look at the mess I was in. I had to survive; I had to find a way. Well-meaning people threw a lot of spiritual bullshit my way, making comments like, "Well, if it's supposed to be it should be easy." What a load of crap! The thing is, all of these people had never done anything other than work for someone else, and yet they dared to sit in judgment on what I was doing. I was angry and hurt, and yet I kept moving forward, one step every day, one step even if it didn't lead to anything.

I kept writing letters and sending emails to Hillary Clinton and people like her: I kept writing, I kept doing. I just didn't know how to quit.

It took an enormous amount of energy to keep going. I had to pull on something so deep to keep on going. I had to pull on pure truth and faith, as that was all I had left. I didn't have time to doubt or to take care of my own personal needs. I pushed relationships aside and dug down and just kept slogging forward. I had to find a way. TRUITY had become even more important than my own survival.

2003, a Year to Remember

What a time! What a life! What on earth has this all been about? Just as with my friend, I was about to undergo a period of what would appear to be devastation and destruction that would have people running from me, wondering if I was the harbinger of doom. Let me recap a little on the last year.

During the last year I had to face losing my first company, after being left in the lurch by a major organization that had agreed to take on my product line, then keeping on in TRUITY tradition, being superwoman. In the last months I have rewritten the whole business plan and gone out into the marketplace seeking venture capital. I knew I had a short time limit. There was only so long I could exist on the little cash I could scrape together. However, believing in God we trust, I simply kept my head down and kept going in the direction of the finish line. The last months have been so disillusioning; I have found myself wondering just what God wants from me. I have kept on, developing the company profile and products, I have marketed those assets to the "right people," and yet we still get this hiss and roar syndrome, where things look so positive and then end in nothing, just like with the venture capital. When I set out to raise the money, I thought, well, if it's meant to be it will happen. But you have to do the hard work to support it to happen, and so off I went, with only faith in hand and trust that the way would be shown.

In the first months after Christmas, I had fifteen companies approach me with interest in financing. The proposals were so varied and covered all manner of inclusions. Some wanted equity, and others just wanted to invest; some wanted security in cash at the bank and others wanted nothing. Finally, I settled on a company called Venture Capital Group in London.

CHOICES BY T.B HUMAN™

Predators on Mayfair: Monopoly Was Never Like This

Hi, News Team: Small businesses being destroyed by predators on Mayfair. (London) Earlier this year I went outside Australia to look for venture capital for the rebirth of TRUITY Holdings Pty. Ltd. TRUITY had been through a very difficult couple of years after a major contract failure and had continued with its vision to develop products related to children's education and personal development, aligned with ethics and emotional intelligence. The company's aim is to empower people to cope with what life hands them.

When I entered the VC marketplace through the Internet, I received many genuine inquiries and offers to finance the development of my product line. After due consideration I decided to go with a British company called V**, based in London. Our first discussions related to the financial position of my company. I made it quite clear that we needed funding fast. The venture capitalists assured me six weeks and it would be a done deal. V**'s director spoke to me of ethics and how this aspect had attracted them to my opportunity, and they offered my company two-and-a-half million US dollars, which was to be an equity and investment agreement. I accepted in early January. I was asked to pay a deposit of $15,000 Australian dollars to their associates, Portland Development Group, also based in London, and I was guaranteed in writing that this money was fully refundable if the venture capital agreement did not go ahead for any reason. (it was never refunded!)

The process continued with a completion of due diligence. I received frequent reassurance that financing had been approved and would be swift and there were no problems. Time began to drag out, and V** continued to be vague and noncommittal about a date for closure on the contracts. I received excuses like, "The war has affected our stocks, and we have to put off signing a short time. But we are going ahead; never any doubt." The partners of the group, Mr. Tony P. and Mr. Neal F., were not being clear about anything. I had staff waiting to move from other countries to commence the commercialization of the project, but no matter how hard I tried I could not get a commitment for timing on signing the contracts. I began to get suspicious when my questions relating to the contract were ignored and my phone calls not returned. I could not contact either partner by email or phone, so I went to London, and in the prestigious area just off Mayfair, I found that all the company had was a virtual office and the reality of the situation began to unfold.

The result of V**'s stalling is that both my company and I are in severe financial difficulty and possibly facing liquidation due to lack of funding. V** strung out the negotiations so long that I am facing the point of no return financially.

The crime for me at that moment was I came face-to-face with the possibility of losing twenty years of first-in-its-field research and product development. If it was just some get-quick-scheme I had developed I wouldn't mind so much, but I have invested twenty years into development of intellectual property related to emotional intelligence and the improvement of dealing with life from a moral and ethical perspective. To gain some legal support, I have contacted the British Consumers Affairs and British Embassy, the British High

CHOICES BY T.B HUMAN™

Commission and other media such as *60 Minutes* and *A Current Affair*. Predators such as these should be brought to the public eye and exposed. I had to find another way and work out why whatever I touched kept falling down.

At this point, Mr. Neal F and Mr. Tony P are just ignoring me. They refuse to close on their agreement and at this time have not attempted to refund the money paid to them in good faith. But that wasn't all that was to happen. In the weeks around this time, people I cared about died or were involved in accidents, things were put off or cancelled, and I was left wondering what the hell was going on, more than ever before in my life. This was truly a time to remember. When I look back on the last thirty years, there have been so many challenges, so much self examination, so much exploration of the mind and soul. I have come to a place within my psyche where I feel I fully understand the truth about my relationship to God. Yet I still can't help but wonder what the point of some of the experiences have been, other than it is insight and knowledge to be passed on to those around me. And in that, it has been worth the journey, for life surely has not been boring.

Stark Naked as a Newborn Babe

Well, it's all gone! Only the company skeleton, the products and the knowledge remain. My home, my furniture, my good name, my business are all gone. I sit here in my daughter's house, computer keys clicking, and yet I am happy. It has been the strangest ride, but I know that from here it will all be okay. How do I know that it will all be all right? I trust myself, that's how! I have found my peace, my strength, my belief in myself, and most of all I have finally looked at issues which before kept me floundering around in the dark not knowing why relationships failed or why I chose the people I did to go into relationships with. Recently, a friend helped me face the fact that I began disliking myself at the age of six, when other children began treating me badly. It was at about that age I began to disown who I was, and I truly began to hate the poverty of our circumstances. I began to be angry with myself because I didn't think I was pretty, and the other kids thought I was strange and called me a witch because I was different, even at that age. It took courage to admit that I had become what everyone else wanted me to become in order be accepted and loved.

It was time to stand up and be counted, time for a new beginning, like it or lump it. I admit I am too outspoken at times. I admit I love with passion. I admit I will fight for the underdog. I emphatically believe in honesty, integrity. However, at the end of the day my conscience is clear, so I sleep like a babe. I do believe that God is all-wise, all loving, and that those events which appear to be disaster often are not. Events happen in order for us to grow in understanding and inner strength. Often this is a part of our developing our character in order for us to complete what we have chosen to do in life. I am an avid advocate of the philosophy that it's not what happens to us that counts, it's how we deal with it.

Ultimately, I believe in my vision of TRUITY and what it can do to improve other people's lives and opportunities. The vision is still as strong as the day I conceived the idea. However, my vision of how I will achieve the end result has changed. From the pain of the experience only good can come. In hindsight, I realize that if business had developed the way it was heading, I would have ended up with a life that I didn't really want. I would have ended up with a life that did not fulfill me as a woman and a mother, or a businesswoman. I have made the decision that from here, my own nurturing and fulfillment as a woman are my primary prerequisites for the next forty years or so. After all, that is the foundation upon which I can build a solid and abundant life.

Look Deep Inside

Most of us fear strong emotions. Society would have us believe that to go to the depths of emotion is wrong. People generally find it uncomfortable to deal with and often friends and family are overwhelmed and run for cover when we show them we are vulnerable or afraid or falling apart. In us they see the mirror of the depths of their own emotions that they are afraid to explore, so they use all manner of avoidance in order to escape what is hidden within them. I believe the last two pages are probably the most profound pages I have ever written. Think about your life, your journeys. Can you now think about past events from a different perspective and let things go?

Can you see the blessings which have clarified your belief in yourself? I would hope that little by little every one of you has the courage to look yourself in the eye and know the goodness and the value of yourself as a person. Believe in yourself, question your motivations, feel your fear and let it go. The one thing that holds us all back from achieving greatness is the belief that we are not worthy of it, the belief that we are stupid, or ugly or whatever. You are a reflection of God, and the world you experience is merely a reflection of everything you see within yourself and your beliefs.

When someone talks constantly about the faults of others, I always understand that what they say is very likely to be a reflection of their own fears and weaknesses. There is always a healing of something needed in such a case, whether it's a lack of confidence, lack of tolerance, or the need to control.

CHOICES BY T.B HUMAN™

Every moment of our lives we have choices, but the biggest problem we have is that we often don't know we have them. Our perception is so limited by our previous experience, that we think that is all there is. I can guarantee there are many, many realities out there for you to explore, but the only one worth the journey is the journey to truth and trust. Happy journeys begin with a choice. All journeys are the result of choice, and it's that simple.

When Two Worlds Collide

It's June 2003, early morning, and once again I have awoken from a deep sleep, prompted by my thoughts to add one more chapter to my book. I am so excited I cannot sleep, as I feel the new beginning drawing ever closer. Every now and then the excitement builds in my chest to the point that my heart skips a beat and I feel sixteen once more. Over the last few days I have come to realize just how much our lives can be and are influenced by so many factors. Other lives, other selves, are all just as relevant as the self that is present here in this moment. I believe that relationships reunite, life after life, to complete old alliances with love and understanding.

Past lives, or other life experiences, have played a major role in the person I have been and will continue to become. The problem is, though, that at times life can become confused when we are blending aspects of ourselves. It can almost feel as though we are caught in a void between the two experiences. The feelings and thoughts we have can sometimes be more indicative of another time and place than of this moment. Our lives are a continual blending of all that we have ever been; it is as though we are continually shape-shifting our energy in an attempt to become complete, whatever complete is.

In hindsight, I now see that God or the universal consciousness or whatever you want to call it had perfect timing on everything. My life has, it would seem, run on parallel to the Billy Connolly movie *The Man Who Sued God*. I know without doubt that I had to come home to heal the relationships with my children and grandchildren before I could move ahead. For, in truth, my whole journey has been about realizing that the one thing I wanted more than anything in this world was to be a part of a family, to unconditionally love and be loved in return. The strange thing about this all is that in the beginning I had what I always wanted; it was just that I couldn't see it.

So, God brought me back to take a second look and to nurture myself with the simple things a family brings into your life, like the hugs and kisses of your grandchildren. I still feel compelled to do my TRUITY, of course, but now it's for them and the children who come after that. I pull together my determination and courage and give it another great big energetic push. Still focused but with the benefits of the solid foundations of love, I now move forward. Only one thing is missing, and that is my soul partner. He is still on his way, somewhere. That warped sense of humor of mine somehow says that he will be very similar to my ex-husband, only an enlightened version, I trust. Life has a way of moving full circle, taking you to a new level each time it passes old ground.

CHOICES BY T.B HUMAN™

Are our lives "made in heaven"? Do we have to complete certain aspects of our lives to meet certain people and join together in certain projects or partnerships?

At times I have flashes of insight and feelings which I know are not mine and belong to my partner, whom I have not yet physically met. There is an urgency in knowing we have already had one chance to meet and it has passed, and now the second chance comes. So that I could understand what is happening, I have been blessed with seeing and being aware of the signs. This understanding has enabled me to fulfill many old commitments and release the past and the fears of the future. I must admit sometimes I am amazed at the complexity and yet the simplicity of it all.

Once I might have become entangled in the physical life and the tiny picture and gotten lost in the emotional chaos. But these days when I feel two worlds are about to collide, I get excited and restlessness, like a cat on a hot tin roof. At those times when my life has been about to change direction and I am about to meet another soul that is closely linked to my own, I find my dreams become profound, and my sense of being in two places at once can become quite disorienting. What people don't realize is we are all a part of each other, and the clearer our individual energy becomes the more we are likely to become aware of those other souls that have journeyed through other times with us. Those aspects of ourselves are also searching for us. Life is a wonderful experience, and the nature of life is we will always be brought to a point whereby we are able to see our own reflection in the eyes of another.

This time, I have an excitement within me that is unexplainable. I have a knowing of this time. This person is the one I have searched for since the beginning of time. In the beginning we were one, and now at the end of our journey after sorting out all the unfinished business we have started with other souls, it is now time for us to share each other's lives in the physical. Will he look like I remember? Or has time changed both of us a little, from the dream to the reality of life? The dream contact with this person has been there all my life.

CHOICES BY T.B HUMAN™

There have been times when it was years between the dreams, but I know he has always carried me in his heart just as I have carried him in mine. The understandings of other lives or other experiences have enabled me to become stronger and yet softer as I have grown. I'm finally awakening from the dream that I could have possibly been separate. I still am not sure if past life does even truly exist in the way we tend to relate to it. However, it really doesn't matter. I often wonder, do we simply look at the vast complex interactions which we call history, making a choice now of creation of "Yes, I'll have a little of Joan of Arc, and a little of Columbus, and there's some interesting African energy I also would like to have, and don't forget the ****.

Do we have other lives? Can there be an end and a beginning to our existence? Well, just like you, I am still pondering those eternal questions. In the last years I have seen so many good friends, good people die of cancer long before their time should have been up, while the rat bags keep going, healthy and happy. I have seen people suffer through no fault of their own, including myself, because of unethical business people.

CHOICES BY T.B HUMAN™

I am sure one day I will eventually look back and say, "Is that what *It* was really all about?" Just like you. The puzzle will be complete, but then *It* always was. Life is about to begin anew once more, and finally I have learned to let go and let God, knowing all will be well, no matter what.

Pitfalls on the Path

There are many varied and well-structured courses available today. For the New Age enthusiast there is a smorgasbord of options, most of which have in common the fantastic, we-will-fix-it-in-a-day sales pitch. Some make far-fetched claims that would lead you to believe that if you follow their processes exactly then you will obtain the desired result. Some of these courses do help for a while, and there are a lot of good people out there doing a lot of good work, but there is an enormous amount of ego attached to the majority of the banquet.

The underlying currents and belief patterns attached to a great deal of the information in these courses keep you from returning "home." Throughout time this has been the case. Returning "home" is to be at peace with your life and your reality. In fact, it is to be free from the chains of pain and struggle that keep us suffering a life of hell on earth. Freedom comes from the inside; it is our natural essence in harmony with our mind and soul. It is this learning to detach by choice from the old programs and by awareness of the principles of life, which bring about the healing and the positive changes in our lives. I always teach my students to look for subtleties of energy. Does the person who created the program look happy? Do they live what they propose to teach? Does their energy feel calm and peaceful? Your eyes will tell you the truth when you look, but your other senses can give you clues, too, and you must learn to be discerning.

Many people get caught up in the illusion of past-life energy of a spirit being or guides. Some will boldly tell you they are channeling Archangel Michael, for example. A person really must have a clear energy field for such an interaction, and for most people that is highly unlikely.

However, try telling someone who believes they are channeling some famous energy that it's an ego-based identification and they will eat you alive. People can be and often are more attached to the identity of the guide, or the importance of the technique or the importance of himself or herself, than they are to get down to the simplicity of reality. When we begin to awaken to the fact that there is another reality right here right now, we struggle frantically in a desperate attempt to change our lives. Often, we create dependencies on other people or other people's knowledge or techniques, past and present and from other dimensions. It is a part of the growing, but it is not where we are meant to stay. Growth is a natural progression from one space to another, and growth essentially requires that we look honestly at our needs and motivation every step of the way.

We do have on earth some great teachers right now, and it is these individuals who often walk the humblest paths through their lives. It is time we solved the problem of codependency once and for all. These dependencies must all eventually be acknowledged and released to reestablish the will and the ability of everyone to guide her or his own life and create her or his own destiny.

The Process

Often a person becomes dependent on "the process." Logical processes will always bring us back to what we already know; they do not break the cycle of activity.

CHOICES BY T.B HUMAN™

Our beliefs and the expectations of our society often subconsciously control our lives. The hard part is we often do not know what we believe because we are not taught to be aware of how our body and mind are interacting with physical reality. Our lives are often steered by the questions we ask, and sometimes we are not aware of how much our lives are restricted by the fact we ask limiting questions. It is important to discover how to ask questions of yourself and others that will prompt new options of how to proceed.

Logical processes often simply reinforce and perpetuate subconscious patterns of energy so that they regain control. You cannot grow in consciousness by controlling your responses or by acting like a robot, learning something by heart and repeating it like a parrot. The only way to really change your life is to bring your energy back to feeling the sense of rightness of action based on divine principles. This sense of rightness, this knowing, resides within each one of us. When we become dependent upon one artificial process or another, we reinforce the separation of ourselves from the truth of ourselves. Ultimately, we are all a part of each other.

CHOICES BY T.B HUMAN™

However, some New Age practices and well-known healing techniques, rather than assisting the person to move towards their true potential, prevent them from enjoying a high quality of life, because they keep the person in a head space which creates more and more thought forms that eventually will need to clear. Such practices, while they are often well meaning, subtly reinforce old beliefs having to do with superiority, secret knowledge and codependent patterns of rescuing the sick or needy. It takes self-honesty and self-knowing to become a master of self. It is not something you can buy or achieve in a week.

Self-knowledge, self-clarity, self-honesty or, to use an older term, self-mastery, is available to everyone who wants a better way of life. All it requires of you is self-love and self-awareness. When we learn a specific process and it becomes active, the student becomes single-minded. They become so focused and want to believe, if I do this I will then get to there, and for a while it will seem to work. Changes will happen, but are those changes in line with the inner self-truth, or has the person simply created a new experience?

CHOICES BY T.B HUMAN™

Often when you use a mind technique for the first time it has an impact, so you use it a second time and it still has an impact, but you must think about using it to get a result. Over a period of time the results gradually diminish, and the individual is less motivated to use that process. Eventually it is forgotten and cast aside like a child's toy.

Often at this point, the student will move on and learn another new method that will once again provide a sense of achievement and the illusion of being one step nearer the destination. Have you ever gone out and bought a chocolate cake thinking that the sugar boost would make you feel better? Generally, after consuming it we feel worse, and then have the added pounds to deal with as well. The hidden agenda here is often the need for emotional nurturing. Well, life is like that. We often think we want one thing and when we get it, we find it's not what we wanted at all. The thing we have struggled to obtain has in fact been a secondary – or a blanket need, as I call them. The real issue is beneath the obvious desire or compulsion, and that's what we have to uncover.

CHOICES BY T.B HUMAN™

You have to be a bit like a little fox terrier chasing a rat. Fox terriers are extremely intelligent animals, originally bred for their ability to catch rodents. When a terrier smells a rat, he will chase around until he finds the rat hole and then dig persistently until he either finds the elusive rat or is called away. He will continue digging even if the rat has been removed when he wasn't looking! He just keeps going because it is his nature. It's in his genes; his sense of smell reminds him that he has for generations been trained to find the rat. The smell of the rat is enough to encourage him to think the rat is still there. The danger of a lot of the New Age process and the mental gymnastics people are involved in is that we can be just like the fox terrier, chasing a prey that has long since disappeared. Be aware of your own compulsive acts, and have the sense to understand that if you're behaving this way, it's time to ask yourself what is really going on. What is the real deep need that is not being acknowledged, and what do you need to be fulfilled as a person?

and ultimately ends up with the person experiencing the energy of lack. This lack can manifest as physical exhaustion, financial insecurity, relationship breakdown and abuse, and many other manifestations. People experience this reality simply from their point of focus and their thoughts. I am always reminded that what we think about, we experience, whether it happens or not. Even if a person has more than enough money or possessions, if they are afraid they will not have enough to last, they will manifest the energy of fear and lack and live in that energy, even though in truth it is an illusion.

The Challenge of Faith

If anyone had ever told me life would come to this, I would have told him or her they are crazy! I feel like I have been shafted in every direction that a person could be. I have had an education beyond comprehension! I always said life on a spiritual path is in fact just is like the movie *The Man Who Sued God*. Little did I realize how much life was about to change, how fast it was about to spin me right back to where I needed to be to heal my life and build empowered solid foundations inside of me. Life had turned into a living hell. I was for the first time in my life having to avoid debt collectors. I was feeling desperate for financial help, and all I seemed to manifest were more people who wanted to take me down. It seemed that everything to do with business was about money. Service providers wanted money and appeared to deliver nothing for the privilege. There seemed to be no tangible supply of assistance to help me climb out of the hole I had dug for myself.

I have been through so much of an adventure in the last fifteen years. At times I find it difficult to comprehend all that has happened. Contracts with major corporations disappeared without explanation overnight; I traveled the world with only a few dollars in my pocket, watched my son fight for life after a car crash, and saw friends die before their time. I have been there and back again, while most people are still thinking about it. And I don't regret any of it. Life is for living, and failure only happens when you don't get back up and have another go. I certainly do not consider I have failed at anything I have sought to accomplish. I get knocked down and I get up again; there's nothing going to keep me down. I have faced so many challenges, lost my home, my car, and all my furniture, all of it sold to pay debts and keep me going. Yet I keep going because I believe in the good of what I do, and I believe in what it can do to help other people.

Along the way, I questioned everything about the project, why I had begun, how I was going to continue, how I was going to survive. I applied for job after job and still nothing came to relieve the pressure upon my situation and me. There was no help; there was nowhere to turn and nowhere to go except north. So, reluctantly, I packed my bags, and in the middle of the day headed for Brisbane once more. I cried all the way, the whole four hours of driving. I did not want to leave the kids and grandkids, but I knew they could no longer cope with the devastation which had become my daily life.

Everywhere I turned people said, "Give up, on TRUITY. Give it up before it kills you!" My children could not cope; most of my friends could not cope; only a few stood by me. I had no choice but to go back to the city in the hope that I would find a way to get through. I drove to Lynne's, and of course she welcomed me with open arms. There was a bed on the sofa and a cup of tea on the table. Life was okay. I knew I would get by with a little help from my friends.

Then it was time for her to move on, and I had to find somewhere else to live, so with four suitcases in hand I picked up the phone and called an old friend. Embarrassment and feeling humiliated by my circumstances doesn't affect me anymore. I believe in what I am trying to set free. I believe in what I have created and its power to help others heal. I am just a vehicle for this giant to be born, and if I must be homeless and penniless to get there, well, so be it. I know my dreams will continue to inform me of the future, of people to meet, people to contact and of the dangers of the path I am walking. I keep focused and just keep praying that I will be shown the way to get through and to get someone to open the door for me, so I can begin to do what I set out to do.

Today, despite the hardship, I thank God that I was pushed so far to find what would heal my life, myself as a woman and as a mother. In a moment, I knew life could begin again. I knew in one breath that there was solidity and fulfillment that I had begun to think was never to be found this life. The tide was turning. However, the turning only happened when I let go of the controls and the rigid expectations of what I thought was for me. Life is good, and it will rebuild on solid foundations. I choose to live life to the fullest and still believe everything is possible and everything is probable. I still follow my intuitive knowing, and know that my truth will lead me home.

I am about to embark on the next chapter of my life. Once again, I wait for the funds to be transferred so I can get out there and do what I have set out to do. My passion is to help people to let go of their limits and in doing so stop the violence, through the use and further development of the TRUITY process, its Internet presence and service.

Violence is not always obvious and external. It's not all about how we treat others; it's also about how we treat ourselves. Violence has many faces. It could be the government, which holds control over people's lives; it could be the attitude of one person to another; it can be physical, mental or emotional. It can be situational, cognitive, or even imaginary. Long ago I

CHOICES BY T.B HUMAN™

realized it was impossible to personally help everyone who needs it. This is why I decided to clone myself in a product that could do the job without relying on me to be there to do it for him or her. I have far too much else to do this life and there just would never be enough hours, not in my lifetime. So many people need help; however, I believe that we can begin to constructively change their futures by expanding their ability to choose constructively.

The results will hopefully be that the generations which follow will benefit in ways that we could never have imagined. Who knows? In a lifetime or ten, maybe, just maybe, I will have contributed to peace on this earth. Once again, the venture capitalist who promised me the earth and shook my hand on it has gone underground. But what he showed me is what can be done on a promise; I have achieved the impossible in the last year with no money at all, not even money to live a lot of the time. I lost my car about eight months ago; I never thought life would come to this.

CHOICES BY T.B HUMAN™

Yet I hold my head up high, and pay a few dollars a week on each of my bills, and just keep going. I haven't been able to get a job; I guess no one wants to hire a 51-year-old genius. So, I just keep going, on faith, on knowing what I have is needed. I just keep going. I don't know how I would have coped if it hadn't been for my friend and his children. They kept me here because they needed me, and sometime when life is that bad, being needed is the main thing which enables us to draw strength from some hidden reservoir deep inside of us, to give to others, to give love to those who have been hurt by life more than you have. It's an amazing thing to look at your own troubles and see how tiny they really are, and just keep on, being there, being the strength and the compassion for the healing.

The last months have been quite an education, but somehow in the midst of chaos, somewhere in all that, I found an even deeper level of peace and faith in what I am doing. I found a peace within me which is so tangible and so strong that now I don't struggle with my destiny, I just step forward into it.

CHOICES BY T.B HUMAN™

If I had not come to Brisbane and lived with my beloved friend and his family I never would have completed what I had to do. Then, the moment I reached completion on the new evolution of TRUITY. One and one really do make three. When I moved in with my friend I became a mom again, taking on his son as my son. And life begins anew.

All karmic debts paid. I wonder what's next on the agenda? Ah well were they paid? Watch out for book of Choices 3 coming out soon.

God bless, 2003 T.B. HUMAN

CHOICES BY T.B HUMAN™

Endorsements

"Every now and then you find someone who has the courage to truly and creatively challenge convention, and the author is one such person. She has a vision, passion and a dream, and wanabelong.com is both the epitome and the realization of her dream. I admire her courage, her tenacity and her creativity and know she is a catalyst for change that the world so desperately needs."
CR Jan Strom, Deputy Mayor, Coffs Harbour City Council, 2003. Best of luck, too! Regards, Jan.

RE: Book of *Choices*, by TRUITY
I have received a printout via my friend Ron's e-mail address. Currently about halfway through and loving it so much. I found out about you and the book through a friend in Melbourne, who happened to be at a BBQ and saw your book lying around at someone's house and opened it up –and then couldn't put it down!! He recommended it to me and I had such great difficulty everywhere trying to get a copy and finally I managed to track you down. It's such an inspiring read and truly

CHOICES BY T.B HUMAN™

a great reminder for me when I sometimes get a bit lost in "the world."
Thank you, and I am sharing it with other souls to benefit from your journey of life.
Namaste and a very big thank you, Sandra May Hudson, Australia.

~~~

Lesley, your TRUITY'S Book of *Choices* has changed my life forever. I am forever in your debt. Mathew, of Sydney, Australia.

~~~

Monday, February 16, 2004, 2:50 pm
just a quick note to let you know I have reviewed your new website and must express my joy at realizing you have not given up on your vision to change the world for better. I understand all that you have had to endure over the two years I have known you and become familiar with Truity. The fact that you have not given up demonstrates a standard of tenacity and self-belief that will drive you to achieve your vision. I am more than happy to offer my contributions in a number of areas to help you achieve your goals.

CHOICES BY T.B HUMAN™

TRUITY is a beautiful blend of principle-based vision and mission with a business that can create wealth. I look forward to seeing this grow. Well done!
Brian Clark, General Manager, Franklin Covey Australia, Pty Ltd, Brisbane, Australia.

~~~

,
What a wonderful vision you have. You pack such punch and express yourself beautifully. Your website delivers a powerful message so beautifully. Continued blessings in ALL that you do in loving peace.
Grace Shanti Fields.

~~~

The author T.B. HUMAN is a highly evolved and incredibly active individual; she is an inspiration to all who know her. She teaches and promotes self-awareness and taking personal responsibility for ourselves and our planet. I have known Lesley for seventeen years and I am astounded by her drive and dedication to stand in integrity, something so desperately needed in the world right now. She is a

CHOICES BY T.B HUMAN™

woman of great wisdom and endless courage. Much love, Sally Yasukawa
Tao Way of Life, Australia.

~~~

1999. "It's all green lights for TRUITY. Best of luck. Dr. Wayne Dyer," Author of *How to Get What You Really, Really Want*, *The Power of Intention*, *Everyday Wisdom*, and other books.

~~~

For more information, or to purchase products please visit:

www.authortbhuman.com

www.ingramcontent.com/pod-product-compliance
Lightning Source LLC
LaVergne TN
LVHW051040080426
835508LV00019B/1628